Celebration of Breath

CELEBRATION
OF
BREATH
(Rebirthing, Book II)

OR

HOW TO SURVIVE ANYTHING
AND HEAL YOUR BODY

SONDRA RAY

Celestial Arts
Berkeley, California

Celestial Arts
P.O. Box 7327
Berkeley, California 94707

An Introduction to Rebirthing for Health Professionals is reprinted here by permission of the author, Eve Jones, Ph.D.

Portions of *Heal Your Body* are reprinted here with permission of the author, Louise L. Hay.

Cover design by Colleen Forbes after a concept by Kaela
Typography by H.M.S. Typography, Inc.
Printed by Delta Lithograph Co.

First printing, April, 1983
Manufactured in the United States of America

Library of Congress Cataloging in Publication Data

Ray, Sondra.
    Celebration of breath (rebirthing, book II), or,
How to survive anything and heal your body.

    "Suggested recordings and tapes": p. 173
    1. Self-actualization (Psychology)   2. Consciousness.
3. Health.   I. Title.
BF637.S4R39 1983   131   83-1770
ISBN 0-89087-355-0 (pbk.)

1   2   3   4   5   6   7   8   9   10   88   87   86   85   84   83

Dedication I

I dedicate this book to all of you Rebirthers in the world who have committed yourselves to this work, who understand the spiritual purification that this process brings and the purity of consciousness required on your part to initiate someone into the next levels of their spiritual path. To those of you who have dedicated your lives to this work for God and who treat it with the respect that it must have, I salute you in gratitude. May this book make your work easier by helping to prepare your clients and by aligning your own thoughts about Rebirthing with those of us who have written here.

Dedication II

To my great friends and colleagues who helped me write this book:

> I have unending appreciation
> love and respect for you!
> You constantly enhance my
> life and the lives of many
> with the quality of your
> love and the excellence of
> your work. Working with you
> has been, and continues to be,
> ecstatic for me. I treasure
> your very existence on this
> planet every day of my life.
> The health of a country is
> determined by its Saints.

Acknowledgement

I acknowledge my friend and colleague, Vincent Newlin, for the title of this book. He has also written some Rebirthing poetry near the end of the book. The title is appropriate, since most of us and our clients who really stuck with Rebirthing are now really celebrating life! Rebirthers for several years have been after me to write a new book about Rebirthing, since my first book, which was written with Leonard, was written at the beginning of the Rebirthing movement, and things have improved a great deal. Rebirthing has become easier, lighter, definitely less dramatic and a lot more fun than it was in the beginning, because all of us who began it and teach it are easier to be with, lighter, less dramatic and a lot more fun as a result of getting rebirthed for years. Our thoughts about the process have also changed.

You who are beginning now have the advantage that you can probably master it a lot faster than we did because we are now clear enough to teach it better. You might say that we finally got out of the struggle and into celebrating.

My Prayer For This Book

Oh, please let what I write be something beautiful for God!

Oh Babaji, fill me with the truth.
  Don't let me be run by the ego
   Let me be a perfect channel for you.
    Guide my words.
     Become my body.
      Become my brain
       and, especially,
        become my breath.
         O, be my rebirther
          Be my very breath
           Breathe life inside me
            so that I can
             Eliminate death!

My Love Letter to You, the Reader

It is my extreme pleasure to introduce you to the world of Rebirthing. I feel honored to have been present at the very beginning of the Rebirthing movement, and it is one of the thrills of my life to share it with you. Leonard Orr, the founder of Rebirthing, now prefers to call it Conscious Breathing. Bobby Birdsall, another one of those at the beginning, now calls it Motivational Breathing. I am still slightly addicted to the original name, Rebirthing. I like it. That is the truth for me. I wrote an earlier book on Rebirthing called *Rebirthing in the New Age* with Leonard. It was written at the beginning of Rebirthing when we "pioneers" were exploring it, were awed by it, and were trying to understand it.

Now it is time to write about it from a new perspective. After seven years, I feel even more in awe of it, even more excited about it, and even more committed to it. It never gets boring to me. I feel that the deeper you go into the spirit of it, the more interesting it gets. I can only say I want everyone to have the experience. I want everyone to know how it can heal the body, how it brings joy and happiness out, how it increases aliveness and has a youthing effect on the body, how it increases psychic ability and develops intuitive power, how it releases old hurt, pain and misery, and how it increases love and prosperity. Who would not want to have the experience? Who would not want to live longer? (Only someone who was miserable and hated life— and yet Rebirthing is here to release the misery and hatred so that you will want to live.)

There is no end to Rebirthing. It is Infinite, ongoing, and eternally enhancing longevity. It can lead to an ultimate goal: becoming a true spiritual master—even giving up death and learning to dematerialize and rematerialize. It depends on how far you want to go, how long you want to live (which is up to you, you know).

Why should we ever stop rebirthing? I cannot imagine. I have been doing it seven years and have been feeling better and better. Who does not want to feel better and better? (Only someone addicted to pain and suffering and the payoffs for it—and yet Rebirthing is here to heal the addiction to pain and suffering.)

Why not try it? There is nothing to lose except misery, pain, suffering and death. There is a miracle available, and that is the total healing of all your negative conditions. There is even complete peace of mind available, and the end to all your problems. *But* it is up to you. We have been given the Holy Spirit to purify us. Conscious Breathing is a way to receive it with respect and let it heal you. It takes some spiritual work along with it, i.e., consciously raising the quality of your thoughts and changing those thoughts you have that produce misery, pain, suffering and death. This goes hand and hand with Conscious Breathing. Your Rebirther will help you with this. Your Rebirther is your breathing coach. Ultimately you will be rebirthing yourself. In the beginning, however, you should not try to do it alone.

Rebirthing originally started, it was thought, to heal the birth trauma (see *Rebirthing in the New Age).* This *is* a major part of it. However, we have learned that it is really a spiritual purification process, and letting go of the birth trauma is only one part of that much greater, all-encompassing process of going for God.

certain types of breathing, or you can go through many initiations with Masters around the world and learn their breathing practices. I am for anything that works. I have tried many things and Rebirthing works best for me. I also meditate, pray, chant and study with the Master. I like it all. My love for Rebirthing in no way diminishes any other spiritual practice. For me, living in the Western world, this is the most practical and effective.

If you feel you can't do Rebirthing because you don't have a Rebirther in your community yet, there are ways of drawing one to you. You can affirm that one will move to your community; or you can go and get rebirthed in another city and become a Rebirther yourself.

Love
Sondra Ray

P.S.

To The General Public

One of the things about this book that delights me is finally to be able to share my new understanding of healing the body (especially Chapter II). Having been a nurse, I am thrilled to get clear on these points about spiritual healing after all these years.

To Professionals

If you are a professional (scientist, therapist, doctor, etc.) and would prefer a more comprehensive scientific approach to the subject of Rebirthing, I think you will be very pleased with Dr. Eve Jones *Rebirthing for Professionals* in the Appendix. Tapes can be ordered of this lecture. When I played this tape recently to my group of Rebirthing students in New York City, they just cheered. As a nurse with a masters degree myself, I feel this tape is excellent, and since I do not write this well scientifically, I appreciate Dr. Eve Jones for her contribution.

To Rebirthers

I hope you will study the Appendix for Rebirthers carefully. It contains an update on some research, a way of understanding the scientific aspects of Rebirthing. Also, I know you'll like my new interview forms for clients (which you can order).

I madeup a list of all rebirthers by state for a directory, but by the time of publication most of you had moved and/or were working on the road. Therefore I'm listing the 800 numbers. Please report in to this number and to Rebirth International with your current address and phone number so we can refer people to you who want to get rebirthed.

Contents

Foreword by Fred Lehrman

READ THIS FOREWORD!

Many people have the habit of diving into Chapter One without pausing to take a breath. This Foreword is important; in Life, breath *is* the foreword. We must inhale before we speak.

You are breathing now. Begin by recognizing, honoring, and enjoying your experience of breathing. You've been doing it since birth; that's when you learned how. It was your first *new* activity when you entered the outer world, the atmosphere. It was the driver's license for your physical body.

Let's start by observing something:

First, hold your breath for a moment and notice how it feels to do that. You will see that your mind keeps going while your identification with your body stops. It is a slightly *disembodied* feeling.

Now, start breathing again, but focus the breath in the abdomen, so that your stomach expands and contracts but your chest stays still. Notice how your mind watches your body, how you experience yourself on two levels at once, observer and observed.

Finally, start to breath gently into the heart area, so that your whole chest moves as you breath. Let the abdomen stay still while the chest rises and falls. (This is a quieter form of how you would be breathing if you had just finished a race; it is how your body breaths when it *wants* air.) Relax your shoulders.

Notice now how your mind and body become one experience. This is what we call *embodied spirit*.

The words *spirit* and *inspiration* come from the Latin *spirare*, to breathe. "AND GOD BREATHED INTO THE DUST THE BREATH OF LIFE, AND MAN BECAME A LIVING SOUL." Most of us, to some extent, remain partially disembodied all our lives. If we learned to breathe under conditions of fear, pain, and confusion at birth, and have been continuing since then with no vacations and no refresher courses, we are probably not breathing as well, or as easily, or as pleasurably as we could. This book is about restoring your birthright to a pleasurable embodiment. That is why breathing and the science of Rebirthing are synonymous.

There are, to be sure, other approaches to freeing the breath. Yoga teaches discipline, power, and calm. Running strengthens and deepens our oxygen intake. Singing coordinates our breath with our emotional expression. But only Rebirthing lets the breath be our guide, our teacher, our deeper self. Rebirthing is surrendering, saying YES to our own life force. We let the breath find its own natural rhythm, shape, and depth. We give the breath full reign over our mind and body, bringing them to harmony and integration with one another. It is exciting, it is overwhelming, it is an incredible relief.

Imagine having driven only one automobile for your entire life. This is your car, and you know it well. It gets you around alright, but it uses a lot of gas, needs frequent repairs, and doesn't handle very well. But you're quite used to it.

Then one day a friend joins you for a drive in the country. As you start to pull out of the driveway, your friend observes that you've neglected to release the emergency brake. When told this, you are baffled. "The emergency *what?*" You've never heard of it before.

So your friend reaches over and shows you how. It is very simple. Now you touch your foot to the accelerator, and the car

LEAPS forward! It takes a few seconds to get accustomed to the new feeling, but the revelation is permanent. Driving is suddenly more fun than you ever imagined it could be (not to mention the savings on fuel and repair bills).

Rebirthing is just like this. The "emergency brake" is in the unconscious suppression of the breathing mechanism. Once released, everything starts to work better. But each person must discover the feeling for him or herself. Your rebirther is a friend who has learned how to trust and let go, and who can accompany and support you as you discover your own inner freedom.

The essence of the free breath is not in quantity, in breathing more, or harder, but in the quality of your subjective relationship to the act of breathing itself. The boundary between volitional, controlled breath and the spontaneous, automatic impulse to breath is brought together, seamless. Each breath is a unanimous action of body, mind, and spirit. With this experience, all levels of our existence come into harmony, and a true foundation for ease and pleasure is finally in place.

As you read this book, remember to enjoy and celebrate your own aliveness and presence. In other words, *let yourself breathe this book*. While breath may be the Foreword to Life, in this case it is also Chapter One and every page thereafter.

Fred Lehrman
Thanksgiving Day, 1982
New York City

1

Definitions of Rebirthing

Leonard Orr, founder of Rebirthing:

As new yoga, Rebirthing is not a discipline. It is an inspiration. It is not teaching a person how to breathe, it is the intuitive and gentle act of learning how to breathe from the breath itself. It is connecting the inhale with the exhale in a relaxed, intuitive rhythm until the inner breath, which is the Spirit and source of breath itself, is merged with air—the outer breath.

The purpose of Rebirthing is to remember and re-experience birth. The experience begins a transformation of the subconscious impression of birth from one of primal pain to one of pleasure. Effects on life are immediate: as negative energy patterns held in the mind and body start to dissolve, "youthing" replaces aging, and life becomes more fun.

Denise Gilman, Certified Rebirther:

Rebirthing is a safe and gentle breathing process that releases accumulated negativity back to and including birth. Through this process, unwanted behavior patterns are revealed and released, and the heart opens so you can receive more love, peace, and abundance. Rebirthing is a powerful healing tool on mental, emotional, physical and spiritual levels. A Rebirth Training is a wonderful way of being introduced to rebirthing, continuing your rebirth process, or applying the training toward becoming a professional rebirther.

2

Spiritual Enlightenment

In order for this book to make sense, and for Rebirthing to make sense, and for life to make sense, it is crucial to understand the following:

1. Spiritual enlightenment: Having certain knowledge of the Absolute Truth.
2. Absolute Truth: Something that is always true for everyone in all space and time.
3. The Absolute Truth is: THOUGHT IS CREATIVE.
4. Thought is creative means: Your thoughts produce results; positive thoughts produce positive results; negative thoughts produce negative results.
5. The way to change your life: Change negative thoughts to positive thoughts by the process of affirmations. An affirmation is a positive thought that you consciously chose to immerse in your being by the process of repetition to produce a new desired result in your life.
6. The only problem: Your subconscious thoughts are still producing results even though you are no longer thinking those thoughts! We all had negative thoughts from

our birth trauma, for example, and these pre-verbal thoughts are still affecting us.

7.   Solution: Somehow these buried thoughts must come to the surface so you can change them. This we have learned to do very easily through rebirthing, by writing affirmations that bring them to the surface, and by being in trainings that bring them to light.

Example

Let's say a baby girl who was hit by a male obstetrician at birth ends up with the thought "Men hurt me." This thought is suppressed more and more until eventually it becomes like a psychic command:

MEN! HURT ME!

This is put out into the world as a vibration and a man will come along and act it out. Then the woman will be more convinced that it is true, and she will say "See, I told you men hurt me." She will make this her reality and believe it. Since whatever we believe to be true, we create, this will happen repeatedly until she is convinced men hurt her. All the time she will believe it is their fault, that they are doing it to her, and she is a victim...when the truth is, she is drawing this situation to her with her own mind based on a thought she might not even know she has. Life will seem awful to this woman, who does not understand why this is going on and continues to hate men.

A rebirther would easily understand how to help this woman change her results. It is a simple process of locating the negative thought that is producing the negative result, breathing the old thought out of the consciousness and using a new thought or affirmation instead.

Example

I forgive my obstetrician for hurting me at birth.

I forgive all men who have hurt me
and myself for drawing them to me.

From now on, I am safe in the presence of men
because I always attract men who are safe
and who pleasure me.

For a lengthy treatice on this subject, I refer you to my first book, *I Deserve Love*, which will teach you everything you need to know about the process of affirmations and changing your reality and getting new results by new thoughts.

3

Rebirthing is Sacred

Rebirthing is sacred. Once I thought it was a scientific process. Once I thought it was a therapy just to heal my birth trauma. I didn't understand it then. But one thing for sure, I *never* thought it was silly. I always knew it was the hottest thing on the planet. That is how I always felt about it, right from the beginning.

Rebirthing is like a sacrament because you are partaking of the Holy Spirit. Rebirthing is making love to God. It is God making love to you. That is what Rebirthing is to me.

Rebirthing is life. It is life-giving. It brings youthing. It brings healing. It brings joy. It brought me everything I ever wanted.

The only reason someone might not want all of that would have to be fear: fear of letting go, fear of danger, fear of death, or, in general, fear of slaying the ego. People may fear Rebirthing because of these things and yet the irony is that *Rebirthing will remove those fears.* Rebirthing continues to take away my fears, and the fears of my friends and clients who have stuck with it.

To me, it is the Ultimate Gift of God.

Rebirthing is drinking the Divine. It is drinking the everlasting nectar of Immortality. It is discovering the Fountain of Youth. It is having the gentle breath of bliss and the power of vitality charging the body. It is the thrill of thrills and the serenity of infinite peace at the same time.

In this simple breathing process, one can permanently release tensions in the body, symptoms of pain and disease, fears of failure, fears of success, fears of love, fears of death, and the beliefs and programming of old age.

It will wash out misery.

It is the Ultimate Cosmic Bath.

Rebirthing is for everyone. No matter who you are or where you are on the path, it will take you higher than you ever thought you could go. You will enter the Banquet Hall of Eternity. You will wonder how you ever lived without it. You will drink the everlasting nectar of joy and your heart will awaken with eternal passion.

Rebirthing is something you will want to do for life. Eventually you can rebirth yourself with no problem at all. Initially, you should plan on having at least ten sessions with a rebirther of your choice, who will eventually teach you to rebirth yourself when the time is right.

You will hear people talk about dry rebirthing, wet rebirthing and group rebirthing.

Dry rebirthing is done lying down on the bed or floor next to your rebirther, who guides your breathing.

Wet rebirthing is done in a hot tub or bath tub, using a snorkel and noseplug to breathe as you float face down in warm water, in the fetal position.

Group rebirthing is done in a large room where a group of people (who have been well prepared) lie down together with the guidance of a Certified Rebirther or other very well-trained and experienced rebirther.

It is best to start out with a series of dry rebirths in private sessions with the rebirther of your choice. You should continue dry rebirthing until you have worked out the bulk of the birth material and a breath release has occurred. Then you can begin wet rebirthing and, eventually, rebirthing yourself.

The first year that you begin rebirthing, it is very important and very helpful to participate in on-going seminars that are related to the Rebirthing process. These include rebirthing seminars, the One-Year Seminar (which meets monthly), the LRT (Loving Relationships Training), or Six-Month or Ten-Week Programs where available. All of these will assist you in your understanding and acceleration of the process and provide you with a "spiritual family" that is like the family you always dreamed about. Directories are given in the back of this book to help you locate rebirther seminars and trainings.

The way to pick a rebirther is to use your own intuition and pick the one with whom you feel the safest and with whom you have the best "connection." It is good to stay with this rebirther for at least the first four or five times so that trust is established. If you start with a female rebirther, it is also good to try a male rebirther later on, and vice versa. This will help you heal relationships with both of your parents.

Once you get going in the rebirth process, you may now and then experience resistance to continuing it. That is exactly when you need to be rebirthed the most. It just means you are about to have a major healing and your ego is "hanging on." You will find that if you go for a rebirthing when you are stuck in resistance, feeling lousy, having symptoms, or when you are depressed, the *relief* you will have during and after the rebirth will amaze you. You will be delivered from the wasteland of pain and despondency into the Golden Fountain of Ecstasy and you will wonder why you waited so long.

As I always say, "Never postpone your pleasure."

4

Procedure for Getting Rebirthed

I. **Preparation for Rebirthing**

   A.   Read this book.

      1.   For further study also read the earlier book on Rebirthing called *Rebirthing in the New Age,* especially the chapters on:

            Spiritual Psychology

            The Rebirth Experience

            Physical Immortality

These concepts go together and it is important to grasp all three in order to get the maximum value from Rebirthing.

Read that book, keeping in mind that it was written in a technical way for Rebirthers.

      2.   If you plan to become a rebirther, please study *Rebirthing in the New Age* carefully.

      3.   Further, read *Rebirthing: The Science of Enjoying All of Your Life* by Phil Laut and Jim Leonard.

   B.   It is often advisable to re-read these books again *after* your first or second rebirth. It will make a lot more sense to you; and you will be surprised how much unconsciousness you might have had the first time you read it as compared to the second time.

C.   Attend a Rebirth seminar, a Rebirth training and/or a Loving Relationships Training in your area.
1.   A Rebirth seminar is simply an introduction to Rebirthing and is given in the evening, lasting a few hours. There could also be day-long seminars.
2.   A Rebirth Training is a more elaborate affair (usually week-long) where you have an opportunity to participate in a rebirth process from the point of view of a rebirthee, observer, and potential rebirther.
3.   There are longer programs if you want a career in Rebirthing.

D.   The LRT (Loving Relationships Training) is a weekend workshop with emphasis on how your birth affects your relationships and covers everything we have learned about relationships from the rebirthing process.

E.   Read the following for further preparation.
1.   *Birth Without Violence* by Dr. Le Boyer (Very good to read aloud)
2.   *The Secret Life of the Unborn* by Dr. Thomas Verny (Excellent)

F.   Write affirmations for even further preparation to make your Rebirthings easier.
1.   Do the ones in this book and those in the back of the chapter "The Rebirth Experience" in *Rebirthing in the New Age*.
2.   Your rebirther will give you specific affirma-

tions pertaining to your particular birth scene and family patterns.

G.   Commit yourself to continue the process as suggested (see following pages). Once you open up, it is important to follow through so that you won't be walking around "half rebirthed."

H.   Understand that spending money on yourself is the best investment there is. Budget "self-improvement" into your budget, knowing that it will raise your prosperity consciousness.

P.S.   If you follow this simple plan and the rest of the suggestions in this chapter, you will find Rebirthing more pleasurable, because you will have enough information to reduce any fear you might have and you will be "activated" enough that you will be very ready ("ripe," as we say).

II.   Find Yourself a Rebirther

A.   If there is any problem in finding a rebirther or Rebirthing Seminar, contact:

REBIRTH INTERNATIONAL
800-641-4645, extension 232.

B.   Among the rebirthers in your area, use your intuition to pick one with whom you feel safest and with whom you have the best "connection." (You can change rebirthers if you like.)

1.   Have at least five rebirths with the same one in

order to establish trust. (The best is to go for ten with the same rebirther.)

2. If you started with a female, switching to a male after awhile is beneficial, and vice versa.

III. Commit Yourself to Complete the Process

A. It is important to have at least ten rebirths. After that you will want to continue forever.

B. It is recommended that you complete dry rebirthing to the point of a Breath Release, then go on to wet rebirthing, and also experience Group Rebirthing at some point.

C. The final step is learning to rebirth yourself.

D. Perhaps you would even make a good rebirther. Rebirthing is one of the most personally rewarding careers I know of.

IV. Support System and Related Seminars

A. During your first few years of Rebirthing, it is very important to have a support system.

1. It is highly recommended that you join a spiritual community that understands the process completely.

2. The recommended approach is to:

a. Join the One-Year Seminar, an on-going group devoted to rebirthing and the healing of the "five biggies." This group meets once a month for a year.

b. Join the "OHANA" or "LRT Family," a group of people who have taken the LRT several times and moved on to the related graduate seminars for the purpose of clearing relationships and studying how one's birth is related to relationships.

    c.   Join a Six-Month Program

B.   For further spiritual work, you might want to connect with a spiritual Master who can guide you, exquisitely, on the path of spiritual Enlightenment. Let God lead you to your personal spiritual master. Many rebirthers feel guided by Babaji, the Yogi Christ of India.

    1.   **Consider reading the book *The Autobiography of a Yogi*, especially Chapter 33, which is about Babaji, The Yogi Christ of India. Also read Leonard Orr's book on Babaji, *Physical Immortality*, published by Celestial Arts.

    2.   If you are interested in connecting with him, I offer you his address:

        Shri Shri 1008 Shri Bhagwan Herakhan Wale Baba
        P.O. Herakhan Vishva Mahadham
        Via Kathgodam Dist. Nanital U.P.
        Pin Code 263126   INDIA

    3.   Prepare yourself to go to him. Before you go I recommend you surrender to the Rebirthing community. This will make it a lot easier on you.

It is *very important* that you are aware of the fact that pieces of your birth experience will come up (surface to consciousness) for years. In other words, once you have "opened up" in your first rebirth, memories will be stimulated to awareness for several years. So the appropriate thing to do is to keep on getting rebirthed in order to release them.

For this reason, it is *not* recommended that you stop rebirth-ing after a couple of rebirths. This is an on-going process. Once you have begun to open up in rebirthing, there is a lot more spiritual force behind your thoughts, and they manifest more quickly and more powerfully. Once you begin to breathe more, it is imperative that you learn to change all your negative thoughts into affirmations quickly. Otherwise your negative thoughts will manifest in the universe and produce negative results with more power. Continuing the rebirth process is the way to handle this situation.

Reviewing the related seminars frequently will also accelerate your process.

As a Certified Rebirther, one of my responsibilities is to help maintain the quality of rebirthing in the world. One of the ways I do that is to remind people of the above, and to remind you to continue the process faithfully for your own well-being.

I have found, however, that even after you learn to rebirth yourself, it is a good idea to be rebirthed by another rebirther quite often. It is usually true that you can get more value with another person present to guide you because the safety factor enables you to go deeper and farther. Once you have learned to rebirth yourself, please remember to do it from time to time with another rebirther.

Never let money problems stop you from rebirthing yourself frequently. You can easily "trade" with someone else who understands the rebirth process: You rebirth that person for an hour and that person rebirths you for an hour.

I have never found anything to spend my money on that is so valuable. And the more I got myself rebirthed, the more money I made. Forty to fifty dollars for one session is very reasonable, since it usually takes about two hours. And, since you can learn to rebirth yourself, soon you will not have to pay for it at all.

A session is usually done in a reclining position, so that the body is relaxed. In other words, dry rebirthing is done with your clothes on, lying next to your rebirther or breathing coach. Rebirthers charge from $1 to $100 per session, depending on their years of experience, their self-esteem, and your ability to pay. The fee is negotiable.

Here are some affirmations used to facilitate the process. Try writing each one at least once and see how you feel.

V.   Affirmations

1. I am breathing fully and freely.

_____

_____

2. I survived my birth, therefore my parents and doctor, and I myself, love life more than death and choose my survival.

_____

_____

3. My physical body is a pleasant and wonderful vehicle for my full and free self-expression.

_____

_____

4. I am glad to be out of the womb so I can express myself fully and freely.

_____

_____

5. I now receive assistance and cooperation from people.

_____

_____

6. I am safe, protected by Infinite Intelligence and

Infinite Love; people and things no longer hurt me without my conscious permission.

_____

7. I am no longer afraid of my breath.

_____

8. I have the right and ability to express my hostility about my birth without losing people's love and support.

_____

9. I am now willing to see my birth clearly.

_____

10. Feeling all my emptiness won't destroy me.

_____

11. I forgive myself for the pain I caused myself at birth.

_____

12. Energy and vitality are my birthright.

_____

13. My mother loves and appreciates me.

_____

14. My mother is now glad that I was born.

_____

15. My mother is now happy to get me out of the womb.

_____

16. It was a privilege for my mother to have the honor to bring me into the world.

_____

17. I am the way, the truth and the life. I came through her body and I am glad to be here. The entire universe is glad that I am here.

_____

18. I no longer feel unwanted. The universe rejoices at my presence in it.

_____

19. The universe is singing in my atoms.

_____

20. My mother, father, family and friends are all glad that I was born and that I am alive.

5

Writings by Other Certified Rebirthers

Fred Lehrman

I have two things to say about rebirthing that may be of value to you in your work. The first is to address the questions "Why is our birth experience such a fundamental factor in our lives, even though most people don't remember it?" and "How does birth exert its influence on all our actions?"

Starting with conception, or possibly earlier, our consciousness begins to record all data, whether physical or psychic, that has to do with our survival. Every time we think we are threatened, whether we really are or not, we use that experience as a guide for our future survival; if we felt pain and fear during the birth process, *and we survived,* our mind henceforward knows and believes that pain and fear can be counted on to guarantee our survival. We are then unconsciously compelled, *in our own best interest,* to keep repeating the same sequence of physical and psychic stimuli over and over again, in real or symbolic forms, because we think our lives might depend on it. Even though this makes no sense, it is logical behavior, given the traumas we have endured. For most of us, our birth experience is our basic survival blueprint, the distorted lens through which we see everything. Since this lens is in our own minds, we never notice it's there.

I also want to answer the fundamental question "How does rebirthing correct this?"

When you lie down to breathe, you are doing the simplest and most complete form of meditation. Nothing is added to your basic life functions and nothing is taken away. Following a relaxed, connected, breathing rhythm is the most fundamental way of saying *yes* to life itself. The environment of the rebirth is safe; any resistance is inappropriate and represents compulsive behavior based on past survival fears. As the rebirth unfolds, we begin to see the design of the distorted lens. *Everything and anything* that happens (other than pleasure and well-being) during the rebirth is an aspect of our learned, false, survival strategy. The rebirth process and the techniques outlined in Sondra's books are sufficient and infallible; start anywhere and relax through your fear towards the center. Every time you can breathe freely in the presence of a negative emotion, you are no longer hypnotized or controlled by your patterns. The distorted lens of false survival beliefs no longer clouds your awareness. Gradually, permanently, with each rebirth experience, your consciousness becomes cleansed of how you thought it had to be, and becomes focussed on how it is.

Rebirthing is not in opposition to any technique or practice that is aligned with aliveness. *Rebirthing is simply this: the most natural and complete way to let go of old subconscious beliefs and to integrate safety, trust, and pleasure into your body and mind.*

Robert Mandel

Spontaneous rebirth experiences are as old as man. Whenever anyone surrenders to the universal life force, an experience occurs that the mortal mind cannot comprehend. The ego loses its grip on reality, creating the space for the higher self to manifest its truths. This is a rebirth.

I remember my first spontaneous rebirth. I had never been out of New York City. I was safe within its walls—New York was my womb. One summer I drove out west. Standing in the middle of Death Valley, I found my mind was literally blown away. All that space! No walls! No limits! My body was trembling, tingling, my heart beat fast. I was terrified. Tears poured down my face. My breathing was out of control. Finally, I surrendered completely to the experience, and all that space outside of me became space inside of me. I was the desert. I was the planet. I merged with the universe. Wow! One of the peak experiences of my life!

Nowadays, the rebirth experience is available in a safe, convenient process called "rebirthing." This simple but powerful breathing tool approaches transformation from the inside out, rather than depending on accidental external stimuli. Rebirthing is a means of coming out of the psychological womb, dissolving body armor, releasing defense mechanisms and bridging the gap between the inner world of spirit and the outer world of apparent reality. Completion of the process results in a remarkable purification of mind, body and spirit.

You no longer need to wait for life to bring you your peak experiences. You don't need drugs. You don't have to climb mountains, run in marathons or leap off cliffs. Rebirthing is a peak experience you can have anywhere, anytime!

Phil Laut

If anyone had asked me, before I was rebirthed the first time, if I felt safe in my life, I would have answered yes. After my first rebirth I routinely began to do things I had prevously thought impossible or weird—fast, stay awake for extended periods, talk in front of groups, have satisfactory relationships with almost everyone, enjoy being self-employed—and I realized that for the first time I really *did* feel safe. My mind and body were filled with a pervasive sense of safety and freedom that has not left me since.

The mind has a strong desire to be calm, peaceful, alert, and free from upsetting and disrupting thoughts. Yet this desire is often thwarted. When you get rebirthed, your mind literally breathes a big sigh of relief. Thoughts, memories, feelings and fears that you have supressed for years will be brought up and, through rebirthing, you will have discovered how to let them go in just a few breaths.

Rebirthing is a simple breathing lesson of connecting the inhale with the exhale in a circular breathing rhythm. For many of us our first breath was taken after the umbilical cord was cut. The umbilical cord is the life-support system that nourished you and "breathed" you during your final weeks in the womb. With the cord gone, learning to breathe on your own is a do-or-die situation. The first breath, then, is taken in panic and fear of death. The memory of this experience can prevent you from ever breathing deeply and fully. Rebirthing can be described as learning how to breathe the way you would like to breathe. The first time you did it, you were too busy *just surviving* to learn how to breathe the way you wanted to.

A descripton of the rebirthing experience starts with a description of life in the womb. According to Western medicine, life in the womb begins when a sperm and an egg unite to form an embryo. The embryo is free-floating and not attached to the wall of the uterus until the twelfth week. (Ironically, it is for this reason that there is little fear of hurting the mother by aborting the embryo before the twelfth week.) By the twelfth week, the embryo possesses all of the body features that it will have at birth—eyes, ears, fingers, and so forth and all of them developed before the umbilical cord was formed. This means that you formed your body *yourself*, out of Infinite Intelligence and Divine Energy.

In a rebirthing session, as you begin to breathe and relax, you will begin to experience, flowing through you, the energy that built your body in the first place. Some people feel this energy flow during sexual intercourse, or during meditation or yoga. It is the same energy that you felt in the womb. This energy can also heal your body; in each rebirthing session, the energy will heal more and more of your body. When it heals your breathing mechanism, you will experience what we call a breathing release. It will feel like your body is *being breathed* instead of doing the breathing.

There is another aspect of life in the womb, the understanding of which will make it easier to have satisfying relationships with your parents, your children and everyone else. It has powerful social and political implications as well. During your life in the womb, the transfer between mother and fetus is totally osmotic: *No blood or other material flows between mother and placenta.* It is not uncommon for mother and child to have different blood types. Essentially, the fetus grows its body itself, with the mother acting as the original landlady. The landlady keeps the temperature right, and supplies air and takes out the waste products.

The essential connection between mother and child is psychic, not physical, and it is the same psychic connection (in kind, if not in degree) that all of us have with each other. This means that there is no such thing as "our own flesh and blood;" our bodies are creations of Infinite Intelligence and Divine Energy, not of our parents' bodies. It follows, then, that each person who lives on this planet is of the same family. The human family is one family.

Everyone who has spent time in the womb associates the flow of Divine Energy in the body during a rebirthing session with the time that they spend in the womb, when that energy flowed uninhibitedly. As you breathe and relax in a rebirthing session, the energy in your body will bring to your attention memories of your birth and the time you spent in the womb. Having conscious awareness of a memory, and of the conclusions you made as a result of the incident, is an opportunity to let go of the pain and the judgements around the event and to integrate the experience as a loving event. Another way to say it is that *the conscious awareness of a memory is an opportunity to see the loving intention behind the event.* It is not necessary to have total recall of your birth, though it is certainly possible to remember everything and many people do. When you have experienced the pictures of your birth, you can be certain that you are free of the fear surrounding the event. It is fear that had previously prevented you from seeing the pictures.

If the doctor forced you to breathe before you wanted to by cutting the umbilical cord, you may find that the pain and anguish of being forced to breathe caused conscious or subconscious patterns of rebellion, resistance or distrust whenever someone suggests that you do something. Life can become pretty dreary if you are always distrusting others, yet the memory of the panic you felt when you trusted the doctor to teach you to breathe may stand in the way of trusting. I would like to share these affirmations with you:

1. I forgive the doctor for forcing me to breathe at birth.
2. I forgive myself for forcing the doctor to get me to breathe at birth.
3. It is safe for me to express my distrust.
4. The more I trust people the more I am rewarded.

From time to time, I rebirth someone who was rebirthed a few times before and, for one reason or another, stopped getting rebirthed. Invariably they are delighted to be breathing easy again.

Rebirthing is for everyone. I want to encourage everyone reading this book to experience breathing with a professional rebirther and to stick with it long enough to complete your breathing release. When this happens, you will be able to rebirth yourself successfully. The ability to rebirth yourself is an important addition to a healthy emotional and physical life.

This book is really the story of thousands of people all over the world who are members (officially or not) of the Rebirth Community. We are pleased to have you as a member. Having a belly button is the only entrance requirement.

(I recommend you read the book Phil has written with Jim Leonard: Rebirthing: The Science of Enjoying All of Your Life. *It can be ordered from Phil Laut, 1636 N. Curzon Avenue, Hollywood, California 90046.)*

Jack Szumel

About the only one I was willing to trust, whose hands I was willing to surrender to, whose wisdom I was willing to receive—was myself. Through whatever or whomever I was attempting to improve myself, the bottom line was always me and my own wits. I was always in control. Rebirthing seemed safe to me, since I'm in charge of my own breathing.

It is mistrust of the world and oneself that is healed in rebirthing sessions. Safety is experienced and integrated. The session creates an environment in the body chemistry that uncovers the natural safety of life. Up to that point it has been clouded over by experiences since (and even before) conception that were stored in the body by underactive breathing.

One's approach to life shifts from mistrust to trust as the rebirth effects a change at the cellular level in the body. Results, in the quality of one's physical, emotional, intuitional and spiritual life, are immediate and miraculous. Youthing occurs. Emotions become safe. Families heal. Life becomes a playful, nurturing celebration.

Today, I see rebirthing as the greatest and most profound historical event since the Industrial Revolution. Its impact is hazardous to all the misery in the world.

Rebirthings' simplicity and applicability to all disciplines has allowed it in five years to spread from San Francisco all over the country and the continent, then on to Asia and Europe. We deserve to have abundant, divine lives. It is our divine manifest destiny, our Birthright.

Jack Szumel in Poland

(The following is an edited transcript of a lecture given by Jack Szumel on September 20, 1981, at the Warsaw Symposium on Healing. The conference was attended by eight to nine hundred people, and aired on national television. This was two months before martial law was declared in Poland.)

I am going to speak about the technique called Rebirthing. In Rebirthing we use our central life mechanism—breathing. We find that breathing is like a solvent that cleans the body.

There are five categories of material that are cleansed from the body. The first is the Birth Trauma. Our first breath occurred at birth, and all of the experiences of that birth are stored in our bodies until they are released by breathing.

The second category of materials released from our bodies is called Specific Negatives. These are negative thoughts about life, concluded from our experience at birth. For instance, if you

were born in a hospital such as I was, you may have been sepa-
rated against your will from your mother, wrapped up tight in a
blanket, and not treated as the conscious, feeling, spiritual
being that you were. Perhaps you were born at a time of war.
Humans make conclusions about life from that kind of
experience.

The next area cleaned by the breathing solvent is called the
Parental Approval/Disapproval Syndrome. This syndrome
works very simply, with profound effects on our lives. It begins
at the point we give up being the source of our own love and
power to our parents, or to the primary authority in our early
years, in order to get their approval. As fetuses and infants we
were self-contained, the source of our love and power. Until we
reclaim being this source, we project this lie onto all authority
figures, giving the government, the professor, the guru power
over us.

The fourth category is the Unconscious Death Urge. Take
five deep breaths, paying attention to the energy in your body.
The Unconscious Death Urge is basically the decision we made
at birth about dying. If you were to isolate all of the negative
thoughts you have about yourself and your life, they would
constitute the Unconscious Death Urge.

The last area of material cleared from the body, using breathing as a solvent, is Past Life Experiences. Simply, we find some
people bring thoughts into this life from past lives.

Now, the point of Rebirthing is not to learn to breathe in any
particular way. It is not a yogic practice. The point is to allow
your breathing to heal your body and mind, revealing your
divine spirit. By this I mean for you to realize fully that you are
not your thoughts. The biggest gift I could give you is for you to
realize that we are not our thoughts, and that we merely create
the reality of our lives with our thoughts. In Warsaw now, and
in this Symposium, you are given little food coupons in order to
purchase food. Thoughts are very similar to food coupons. For
instance, a person who makes the conclusion at birth, "There

are not very nice people around me," carries that thought coupon. That coupon will only buy "not very nice people" for that person. Why? Because the universe will always agree with your thought and prove it to be true. That coupon or thought will always purchase the same result.

If you think fire will heal you, fire will heal you. [The previous speaker was a Hindu who performed a fire ceremony.] If you think breathing will heal you, breathing will heal you. The truth is that you in your divine nature are healing yourself, or not, depending on your thought coupon.

During this symposium, I have no technique to offer you. All I have to give you is yourself, because you are the thing that works. We are all Divine Gods creating our Universe with our coupons. For those of you who say, "Oh, nothing works for me," I know nothing will work for you until you see that that is only a thought. You are the thinker of that thought, and can exchange it for one that brings the result you want. The thoughts that you focus on and repeat with your mind will expand in your life. People in New York City who think that there are dangerous muggers there, get mugged.

Will you please take five deep breaths and feel the energy in your body.

United States scientists have just completed experiments on the placebo effect, using open-heart surgery patients. Half the group tested were actually given open-heart surgery for their heart ailment. The other half were told that they were given the surgery but really only were cut superficially on the chest. The results were amazing! The placebo group healed their heart conditions more rapidly and effectively than the patients who actually underwent the operation. Everything in life is a placebo. We are always the actual healer; and as one of the previous speakers mentioned, the only healer is love. So, my Polish friends, we are love; and whatever we think will heal us, we must do. Do what you think will heal you, not with effort, but with love.

In the United States, I laugh at the materialism. "All I need is a Cadillac, then I'll be happy." Then when there's a Cadillac, "Maybe another one will do it," and on and on it goes. People await satisfaction from one thing to the next. Now, in Poland, healing techniques are coming in like Cadillacs. "Oh well, I'll get rebirthed, then I'll be happy." "Someone will lay their hands on me, then I'll be satisfied." "Solidarity will make me happy," and on and on.

Right now a critical mass of Parental Disapproval on Earth is bursting. The focal point is Poland. The only way out is love, and safety with anger, on personal, social, and political levels. Up to this time, attempts to reclaim personal authority or power from governments have been through violence. Poland, on the other hand, has the highest life urge of any country that I have been in. It is also the safest with its anger.

In recent history, the Death Urge has been filtered out of the Polish people to a very large extent. Those who thought they had to die to get what they wanted are dead. Now remain those who are living with humor to get what they want. I ask you to focus your strong life urge on your own family life, choose coupon thoughts that serve you, and create your own happiness. If you are not willing to receive nurturing on this level, your government is never going to give it to you.

I will add that if we create our reality with our thoughts, so then do we create our death or eternal life with our thoughts. I am physically immortal and choose to stay here for thousands of years, until I find something more enjoyable to do. Thank you, very much.

Peter Kane

I chose Rebirthing as my Career because the experience of pleasure and aliveness that the breathing process brings makes it very easy to love myself and my life. There are a few thoughts about this I would like to share with you.

Rebirthing is a breathing process that releases tensions from our breathing, freeing it, and integrating its full potential for use in our daily life. The breathing takes in energy which can be described as oxygen and/or as spiritual energy and life force. The nature of this energy is that it dissolves anything contrary to it. In this way Rebirthing works by dissolving any blocks to the flow of energy in the body and becoming aware of these blocks at their psychological or spiritual source. The breathing and the energy are the links. To open up the breath is to open up the mind, body and spirit. This is a cleansing process. It expands the positive life force, thus creating room to release negatives as well as using the positive energy to purge them, rinse them clean, and provide the strength and aliveness to choose life on a new level. The breath becomes a permanent vehicle for this, and each breath becomes a rebirth.

I call Rebirthing an intuitive science, but it is much more. It is about you and your relationship to your life... your choice for it... your passion!

Lucy Liggett

So many people think that, because the breathing energy of Rebirthing releases negativity, Rebirthing is *only* about releasing negativity. This is not so. Rebirthing is for fun, for joy, for pleasure and for reconnecting with our God-self; for bathing in the pleasure of trusting the God within us. Rebirthing is truly the easy way. Think about this! You create your own reality with your thoughts. Everything you value or focus on will expand. God energy supports you totally in whatever you think. Another way of saying that is Energy follows your thought and manifests through it. If you have the belief that Rebirthing or any other self-help technique is only to release negativity, it will—only there is a catch! If releasing negativity is what your goal is, you will continue releasing negativity and your mind will create more negativity to release for ever and ever.

Rebirthing is much more than many of us dreamed it would be when we first experienced it. It is a most sublime and easy form of meditation and spiritual purification. The simple act of merging the inhale with the exhale of the physical breath allows the inner breath (God Consciousness) to emerge and transmute our outer being; personality, mind, physical body, emotions and behavior become purified. This allows us to claim our true inheritance, which is that we are Divine Beings who have previously suffered from spiritual amnesia. Can you imagine a more fun and pleasurable existence than to live continuously in ease and pleasure? In a God-permeated existence. That is what Rebirthing is about for me.

Another beauty of this spiritual tool called Rebirthing is that anyone at any stage of the path can use it to enhance and expand his or her growth. Limitations are dissolved because the premise of Rebirthing, which is non-judgement and unconditional love, is something we can all come to claim.

An image comes to me over and over again about life—and Rebirthing is about LIFE! It is the image that this song puts in my mind.

> Row, Row, Row your boat,
> Gently down the stream.
> Merrily, Merrily, Merrily, Merrily
> Life is but a dream.

Yes, that is what Rebirthing is about. Going with the stream of life.

Quotations

Judy Dubois

1. *On How Rebirthing Contributed to Her Life*
   "I feel more safe and present in my body. Even when I feel afraid, I know I'm all right."
2. *On Being a Good Rebirthee*
   "Practice self-love. Be loving to yourself no matter what you get: It is *your* program and if it is different from programs of other people in their rebirths, it is never "less than" theirs. It does not have to be like theirs."
3. *On Becoming a Good Rebirther*
   "There must be that willingness to turn the rebirth over to God. You become a channel. It is important not to think that *you* did it."
4. *On Rebirthing and Relationships*
   "Thanks to Rebirthing I'm more able to love myself in the presence of others. My self-esteem is greater than my fear of disapproval."

Diane Hinterman Siddall

1. *On the Subject of Rebirthing and Immortality*
   "The mind is the doorway to your eternality and Immortality... Your breath is the escort."
2. *On How Rebirthing Has Improved over the Past Few Years*
   "The Spirit in Rebirthing in the past was diluted by not focusing enough on the power of the breath and over-focusing on the mind."
3. *On How to be a Good Rebirthee*
   "The 'Way' of rebirthing is to relax into the knowledge that your own true nature is love. Rebirthing is the

physical practice of experiencing your own true nature motivated by a loving intention. Through this knowledge comes the enjoyment of the gift of your own unique life."

4. *On What Has Helped Her to Become a Good Rebirther*
"I feel a deep intimate commitment to my own expansion...I am constantly willing to learn."

5. *On Rebirthing and Relationships*
"Thanks to Rebirthing I don't have to leave to be safe. I can be loved and be safe."

Mallie Mandel

1. *On How Rebirthing Contributed to Her Life*
"I can wake up laughing now! Before I dreaded waking up because I was born early in the morning. They had to use forceps to drag me out. Everytime I woke up I said "Oh No!"
"It gave me a tool for being comfortable in the presence of my entire family."

2. *On Getting Results in Rebirthing*
"Breathing is a tool that only works to the extent that you know how to use it. In other words, one has to not only handle breathing, but creative thought and relationships at the same time.

3. *On What Helps Her to be a Good Rebirther*
"I have an experience of my life being peace with passion."

4. *On Rebirthing and Relationships*
"Since I now take a breath before I react, my relationships are less compulsive and more intuitive. Rebirthing has given me a deeper knowledge of Immortality in my body, and that knowledge has given me a far deeper commitment to each relationship in the present moment."

6

Recent Writings by Leonard Orr, Founder of Rebirthing

This chapter is a summary of some recent writings by Leonard Orr, with a few my comments added.

Rebirthing

Rebirthing, or "conscious breathing," is a physical, mental, and spiritual experience all in one. It is mostly physical and spiritual because rational thought is usually bypassed. The physical part is the connecting of your inhale to your exhale in a relaxed rhythm. The idea is to merge your inhale and exhale so that your breathing feels and sounds like an unbroken circle. Your inhale and exhale should be relaxed and full, not forced. The breathing should not be too fast or too slow. The most important thing is the even rhythm. You can breathe through the nose or the mouth. This kind of breathing is done mostly in the chest, with emphasis on breathing with the lungs instead of the diaphragm or belly.

The spiritual dimension of conscious breathing is the heart of the matter. The purpose of conscious breathing is not primarily the movement of air, but the movement of energy. If you do a relaxed, connected breathing cycle for a few minutes, you will begin to experience dynamic energy flows in your body. These energy flows are the merging of spirit and matter. The state of your spiritual enlightenment and the intuitive guidance of your rebirther is the biggest factor in determining the power of your energy flows. These energy flows we most often describe as "tingling" or "vibrating" sensations in the body. When these energy flows are happening, your body is being filled with pure life energy and your mind and body are being cleansed of tension and impurities.

Rebirthing has the potential for cleaning the physical body and emotional body and nourishing them more effectively than food. Rebirthing can give you a physical experience of spirit, a physiological experience of the human aura.

Breathing in this powerful, productive way is a potential you have always had. People have been sub-ventilating, however, probably because of unconscious fears of stimulating early memories, even back to birth. Rebirthing makes it safe for these memories to come up, if they do. The rebirther will help you release them from your body and change any negative thoughts associated with the memories. In my experience it always feels better to release these memories than to keep them suppressed. Suppressing them causes pain, negative symptoms and disease. Releasing them brings health. One of the greatest benefits from this kind of breathing is that after you learn to do it yourself you have tremendous self-healing power.

Connecting the inhale to the exhale merges spirit with air. It merges the energy body with the physical body in a way that nourishes the nervous system; it cleans blood and relaxes the organs as well as the mind. This spiritual breathing is like a biological experience of God.

The conscious breathing method we are talking about was originally called Rebirthing because any conscious breathing can stimulate birth memories—for the obvious reason that birth is the moment of the first breath. If you study your breathing rhythms long enough you will eventually remember your first breath. It is important to keep doing the process until this happens. This moment, when it occurs, we call the *Breath Release*. It will happen when you feel safe enough to remember and re-experience your first breath. The breath release is the turning point of rebirthing because in that moment the breath mechanism is healed of the damage done to it at birth. Prior to a breath release, people usually are breathing by taking very little air in on the inhale and by forcing the exhale. This sub-ventilation, which most people do all their lives, does not promote longevity. The cells are not getting enough oxygen, and exhaustion and old age set in from forcing the exhale. After a complete Breath Release, a person breathes differently. There is a natural "pulling in" on the inhale and a "relaxing" on the exhale. During the Breath Release there is usually a period of hyperventilation when it feels like someone else is breathing you. This is a very exhilarating experience and will happen only when you feel safe enough to let go completely.

People have often had mystical experiences during this release. My experience is that the Holy Spirit "takes over," and the only thing to do during that moment is surrender complete-ly and thank God you are being healed. People often don't allow themselves this kind of release until they feel very safe in their body; they must understand that there is no source outside them that can kill them and that they are responsible for their own life and death. Understanding the concept of physical immortality and how it is imperative to the rebirthing process is a major factor in being able to let go completely (see Chapter 7).

Sometimes during breathing sessions one may experience some unusual symptoms, such as stiffness of the hands (due to releasing suppressed tensions accumulated and stored in the brain during infancy and also to resisting the Life Force coming in). The body might be pulled into a fetal position temporarily. There may be a lot of sadness coming up, due to the "unlimited sadness" that infants sometimes experience during birth because they were mishandled. Fear may arise while birth memories are being released of feelings during contractions, the actual expulsion, and the early separation from mother. There could be pressure on the body parts as one remembers coming down the canal, and even the smell of anesthesia coming out of the body, where it has been stored from birth.

All of these symptoms appear and disappear in a matter of minutes. All one has to do is maintain connected breathing and follow the guidance of the rebirther, who had already been through these experiences and knows they are very temporary. These symptoms are caused by past thoughts and feelings. A symptom is the manifestation of an old negative thought in your body so that you can release it through your breath. ALL SYMPTOMS ARE THE CURE IN PROCESS. A negative thought, formerly suppressed, is trying to get out. It is much better to go through a few minutes of symptoms in a rebirth and breathe it out than it is to have those negative thoughts suppressed and causing negative mental mass (disease). The symptoms are rarely very painful unless you start making them real. All they really are is thoughts that you can change. Most people, in fact, think of these dramatic psycho-physical memory phenomena as interesting and even fun. The symptom is a real body sensation, but continued breathing rhythm causes it to disappear in a few minutes. Your breath and spirit releases the symptom from your mind and body and you feel free and clear.

Once you have experienced your ability to breathe away symptoms during a conscious breathing session, you can use this ability to heal almost any form of mental and physical sickness. Breathing itself does not cause the symptoms, relaxing does, by permitting a negative thought to manifest that was formerly suppressed. Then more breathing and relaxation will dissolve the symptom and its cause (which was just a thought).

In the beginning of rebirthing you might feel very emotional—sometimes distraught and overly dramatic. One of the goals of rebirthing is to get to a place of peace and emotional balance. This will come. Keep going! You want to get beyond the physical, emotional and mental, up to the Intuitive level.

Spiritual Purification

The idea of spiritual purification is to enrich and fill the mind, body and spirit through simple exercises. If the following exercises are studied and practiced intelligently and patiently, they may cause clarity and victory over all personal problems. They can make people permanently healthy in mind and body. These exercises are very simple and easy to do, but they should be done in small doses because they have the power to induce temporary insanity! By "temporary insanity" I mean letting yourself feel the emotions of fear, sadness, anger, depression, confusion, despair, frustration, and so on. Any technique or exercise, such as fasting, has the power to bring suppressed emotions to the surface and to cleanse them out of the human personality. The cure for temporary insanity can be realized instantly in most cases by repeating, concentrating, or thinking about the following idea: "The Bottom of all Emotions is Infinite Being." Or it is just as true that at the *top* of all emotions is Infinite Being. Infinite Being is order and peace. Infinite being is wisdom, humor, love, common sense and spiritual enlightenment.

The goal is not pain, or even the ability to endure pain. The goal is freedom from pain. I recommend that you take one exercise at a time and experiment with it. I recommend that you start with the one that is easiest for you...and by the time you have mastered the easy one, the hard ones will be easy also. I have found that self-mastery brings tremendous satisfaction. The discomfort of fasting for three days is nothing when it is compared with the joy of accomplishment after completing it.

The discomfort is also nothing when it is compared to the pleasures of eating afterward! To be too enthusiastic about one method of purification (such as fasting or vegetarianism) is fanaticism and unbalanced. All techniques should be used in moderation. *Slowliness is holiness.* Even moderation should be used in moderation. I have found spiritual purification to be fun and very enlightening.

The goal of spiritual purification is to tap enough of man's divine nature to produce Heaven on Earth. A superficial study of the following catalogue of spiritual purification exercises will reveal that they are main themes of the teaching of Jesus, the Bible and all the great world religions. Practicing them in moderation evolves humanity, as well as the divinity of all people.

God has leased us a body—the lease payments have to be made if we desire to keep it. God doesn't require money, he requires the fulfillment of a few simple exercises that demonstrate that we have mastered our own possession. God has also leased us a planet, as the Hopi Indians have been trying to teach us. All thoughts and actions have the power to bring about prosperity or disaster. The lease payment consists of love and respect for Mother Earth and her resources.

The following exercises bring about a cleansing of the physical body and the human mind, and a conscious relationship to Mother Earth, so that our enjoyment of the physical earth is guaranteed. If every person practiced these simple principles, they would manifest Heaven on Earth.

The Basic Spiritual Purification Program:
A Three Year Course in Truth, Simplicity and Love

Eternal Life is the Source of Youthing as well as Aging.

Step 1 — The mind. Write out on paper or record on tape your thoughts, for fifteen minutes — uncensored. Then go through what you have recorded and change all the negative thoughts into positive ones in writing. Do it again. And do it again and again until you feel good. One whole day per week should be devoted to this process until you feel good or high all week. Then you can continue it only one hour per week. You can accelerate this process by doing it every day. If you do it too much, you will have a tendency to get spacey and unproductive or hyper. This exercise should be done every time you feel low or depressed. It shaves off the bottom of each discouragement. It should also be done during spaceyness and at times to find out what the source of the tension is. This exercise will eventually yield total peace and control of your mind, your body and your life. Expose yourself to good literature through books and tapes.

Step 2 — Your breath. The breath is the power of both the human mind and body. Do 20 connected breaths each day — connecting the inhale to the exhale in a relaxed rhythm. Be gentle and conscious on the inhale and relaxed on the exhale. Let go of the exhale so that gravity is causing the exhale — no pushing or holding. Do 10 to 20 spiritual breathing sessions with a well-trained spiritual breathing teacher or rebirther. This should include warm water rebirthing, as well as cold water rebirthing.

Step 3 — Food. Abstain from food for one day each week for one year. It probably should be a week day. Weekend days are often social experiences and therefore they are not good to establish a rhythm. Do only one day per week the first year. Then do two days per week the second year. Then do three days per week the third year. I don't recommend that you accelerate this program because your mind and body likes lots of time and experience to integrate these new food habits and rhythms. It is OK to do half day fasts and to cheat occasionally in order to process guilt and to learn something about the yoga of comfort and pleasure. Liquids are permitted on fast days. I recommend vegetarianism and fruit diets as a normal practice.

Step 4 — Sing the name of God daily. You can chant any name for God, but I have received the greatest value from singing *Om Namaha Shivai*. The purpose of repeating the name of God every day is that it evokes the divine presence and all divine emotions. It is wonderful to remember the name of God constantly throughout the day until it becomes an ever-present thought. This may be the simplest and the greatest technique of spiritual purification.

Step 5 — Physical exercise. I recommend that you walk around your block every day and meditate upon your neighbors for the purpose of loving them all. Be conscious of nature in your neighborhood.

Step 6 — Sleep. Stay awake all night once each month. Meditate on the emotional changes and body feelings. Meditate on the moon and the sunrise. Use the affirmations exercise in step one to process your disturbing thoughts or feelings.

Step 7 — Spiritual community. Participate in a monthly town meeting on your block. The purpose is to realize a spiritual family and friendships as well as to fulfill the basic responsibilities of citizenship. Learn from the great saints on earth.

Step 8 — Hair. Shave your head at least once every 10 years. I recommend that during one year every decade or so, you shave your head once per week for nine months. This cleans your energy body, heals the body and reverses the aging process. It accelerates the youthing process.

Step 9 — Bathing. Water purification is simple and easy. I have had the practice of meditating while immersed in a warm bath tub for one hour per day for many years. Taking showers daily is effective, but I recommend total immersion in water at least once a week. Doing connected breathing while entering the water produces special value, but you can easily experience your energy body, the human aura, by meditating on feeling changes as you enter the water.

Step 10 — Fire. We have taken fire for granted. We use the power of fire in our cars and our homes; it does most of our work for us and is the source of infinite kinds of comforts and pleasures. In India and in Native American cultures, people practice a ceremony of feeding the fire with ordinary daily food as an act of respect and gratitude for what fire does for us. American Indians also sometimes give food to their water sources also to feed the gods of nature. These are good practices.

Step 11 — Manual labor. Physical work is holy. I recommend that you regularly use your body to do house work, gardening, even carrying out your own trash. Working in or on the natural earth produces good feelings and spiritual enlightenment. Farming is the holiest occupation on earth. Body work methods like massage and athletic activities also qualify as manual labor. Receiving massage and body work like Rolfing, Feldenkrais, Alexander, Traeger, Vitaflex, Tai Chi and athletics are all methods of spiritual purification.

Step 12 — Population control. Each person must exercise more responsibility for our reproductive powers. The present population on earth can and should be reduced by peaceful means. You can do it by controlling your own reproductive powers, controlling the population growth on your block, and in your city. The birth-death rate on your block should be counted monthly and annually to make yourself and your neighbors conscious of these responsibilities. As physical immortality becomes more popular, more conscious child bearing becomes important. Unraveling the trauma of the birth-death cycle rehabilitates our ability to appear and disappear on earth by choice.

Step 13 — Money. Winning the money game through intelligent, enjoyable and loving service is a method of spiritual purification. Your rewards in life, tangible and intangible, are directly proportional to the quality and quantity of service you render to your fellow beings on this planet.

The revelations and freedom that will be inspired in you as a practice of these thirteen simple and natural spiritual purification exercises have the power to realize Heaven on Earth. Your personal perfection has been waiting for you throughout all eternity. These spiritual purification exercises will open you up so you can let it in. They will enable you to release all of your negativity. They are fun and enlightening.

(I thank Leonard for these contributions.)

7

Rebirthing, Longevity and Physical Immortality

(I suggest you read this chapter very slowly, line by line, taking time to absorb everything.)

To me, the most exciting and liberating ideas in the universe are contained in this chapter. Mastering these principles is of the utmost importance in helping you relax and feel completely safe in Rebirthing. The philosophy presented here gives you something to think about for a very long time and will promote continual healing in your body. It will give you the opportunity to have the long sought after Fountain of Youth within your reach.

I dedicate this to my Immortal Master Babaji Shri Shri 1001 Shri Bhagwan Herakhan Wale Baba, who I met in this life after I wrote the chapter on Physical Immortality with Leonard for *Rebirthing in the New Age.* I feel that, because I had the courage to write that almost a decade ago when it was still considered outlandish, and because I had the courage to go and surrender to Babaji himself, I have been blessed with mystical experiences that proved to me that it is not only possible to live as long as you want in the physical body (if you have the right thoughts and are spiritually purified) but you can also dematerialize and rematerialize just as the Spiritual Masters do.

The belief that death is inevitable has killed more people than any other cause. There are case histories of people living for thousands of years by practicing simple areas of spiritual purification, but you would never think of looking for them if you didn't believe in the possibility of physical immortality. If you understand the truth that your thoughts create your reality and you have certain knowledge of that, you are enlightened. Taking it further, you will see that what happens to your body is also a result of your thoughts. The trouble is, we all "bought into" the popular belief that you have to die around 70. (A belief is just a group of thoughts.) There are people around who have lived a lot longer. There are even people walking around who look 30 and are much, much older. They will never tell the truth about their age until it is safe. They do not want to be thought crazy and locked up.

Jesus conquered death, and that was the whole point of the New Testament. He was trying to show us we could master our bodies. Few got it. Most people got stuck on the Crucifixion and missed the point of the Resurrection. Jesus took his body with him. He materializes it for certain devotees even now. Babaji materialized his body for one decade to help us in the coming times of strife. He has materialized and dematerialized his body at will for thousands of years. He is available to us in the flesh now, and you can read about him in Leonard's book *Physical Immortality, The Science of Everlasting Life,* and Yogananda's book, *Autobiography of a Yogi.*

There are many books out on physical immortality now. We call this the Immortalist literature. Here are some of them I recommend:

REBIRTHING IN THE NEW AGE
   (Chapter 5)
THE DOOR OF EVERYTHING
LIFE AND TEACHINGS OF THE MASTERS
   OF THE FAR EAST (5 volumes)

AUTOBIOGRAPHY OF A YOGI
STOP DYING AND LIVE FOREVER
BEYOND MORTAL BOUNDARIES (and all
   of Anna Lee Skarins' books)
PSYCHOLOGICAL IMMORTALITY
A COURSE IN MIRACLES

The main point I want to make is that you do have a *choice* about what to do with your body. Jesus said "The power of Life and Death are in the tongue."

It is essential to look at the issue of death and physical immortality if you are starting the Rebirthing process. We Immortalists consider it unethical to teach enlightenment to our students and rebirthees without teaching them how death works. It would be unethical for me to write this book and turn you on to rebirthing without covering this subject. The reason is this.

As you get more enlightened and change your negative thoughts to positive thoughts, you get more energy. As you rebirth and do conscious breathing, you get even more power and energy. You end up with a lot more spiritual force behind your thoughts. They manifest more quickly. If you hang onto the thought "Death is inevitable," then you will have a lot more force behind that thought the more you get enlightened. Since in metaphysics it is known that what you think about expands, your death urge would increase. Then your death urge will become stronger and stronger, so that pretty soon all you would be thinking about is death, and you could kill yourself faster. This is why it is absolutely imperative that you understand that *all* thoughts can be changed. Even your thought that "Death is inevitable" is nothing but a thought! "But," you say, "I see death out there all the time. I know it is real." Yes, but all those people killed themselves with the thought death is inevitable.

The truth is ALL DEATH IS SUICIDE.

People often say to me, "Oh, I wouldn't want to live forever, it is too much pain and misery." I am not talking about living in pain and misery. Again I say, the reason you are in pain and misery is because you bought into the idea of death in the first place! I am not talking about living in an old body either. I am talking about staying at the age you want—looking and feeling good and staying there. If you could have *that* then you might want to stick around. You *can* have that (the Fountain of Youth) if you will surrender to these ideas, change all your thoughts, and experience youthing.

I also dedicate this writing to all the Spiritual Masters, Avatars and Hierarchy in the Spiritual Government who have already transcended the birth/death cycle. You can do this too. All differences are temporary.

I, Sondra, do not pretend to know the highest thought as to how the body will look after mastering these principles completely. I do know there is tremendous and unlimited value in studying the subject of life extension and transcending all limiting ideas such as death. *A Course in Miracles* says that death is the result of a thought called the *ego*. One of the favorite tricks of the ego is to convince you of the thought "Death is inevitable." The *Course* also says "Life is a result of a thought called God." Leonard used to teach us that man has always hated God for putting him in what seemed to be a closed universe from which there was no escape of death. God did not do that. Man was trying to prove there was no God by creating death. Look what it says in *The Door of Everything*, my favorite little book on this subject:

> *The last and greatest evil to be removed from the precious planet earth is satan's evil, death. Jesus said "Verily, Verily, I say unto you, if a man keep my word he shall never see death." Could any talk be plainer?*

It is true that life is everlasting regardless of how many times one lets the body die. It is true that the soul lives on and can create a new body for itself. But, it is also true that the soul is endowed with wisdom and it knows death of the body is out of harmony with the universal law of life. The soul yearns to be exalted to the vibration of the Ascension Attitudes (love, praise and gratitude) so it can travel the way of Saints. In order to travel this highway, it needs a body which overcomes the destructive earth vibrations and is transmutable into light (dematerializing and rematerializing).

When one chooses to die, death does release the weight of gravity and temporarily frees the soul from earth. But it does not change the vibration of consciousness from the human level. (In other words, you do not go to a "higher plane" where you are "better off.") There is no escape from the vibration of yourself except through practiced change of thoughts. Nor does death cause the released consciousness to go to a celestial level. Consciousness, when departing from the body, automatically seeks its own level.

Every lifetime is a new opportunity to be enlightened and annointed with the light and to rise above the trap of death. "For he that is joined to Him that is immortal, will also himself become immortal."

(From the chapter "The Lightning Flash")

To me, this writing clears up the notion that some people have that you would be better off somewhere else. In other words, death is no "solution."

I do know from my own experiences since meeting Babaji and mastering these principles, that the body will become more and more light and angelic as one continues to let go of thoughts · of ego, and as one continues spiritual purification practices, such as *Rebirthing.* This kind of breathing raises the vibratory rate of your cells and puts you into the kind of state that enables you ultimately to teleport, bilocate, dematerialize and rematerialize. One has to break out of the habit of dying and re-incarnating. The way I look at it is this: Once you have worked out the Birth Trauma from your consciousness, why go through another Birth Trauma and have to do it all over again? Why not master your body, breathe out all the death programming, and get your body to look and feel the way you want at the age you want—then go on to become a true master? I feel that one has to love one's body as much as God loves the earth (eternal love). The experience of eternal love of your temple (body) will ulti-mately, I believe, turn your body more and more into light vibration and there will be transmutation of the cells (quicken-ing) to the point that one day you can have a Saint-like body through transmutation.

It is important to realize that YOU ARE NOT YOUR BODY. Your body is in you, the Greater Self. The body is an illusion. It is a reflection of your thought forms and is held together by thought. The vibratory rate of the cells is slowed down enough for you to be "seen." When you dematerialize, you increase the vibratory rate of cells enough to make them move into the One. Reading the *Course In Miracles* and *The Door of Everything* is helpful in understanding this.

The first step in becoming a Spiritual Master is to love your body as much as God loves the earth and to give up the idea of killing it. When you give up the thought "Death is inevitable" and purify your body of that mental construct, then you will be moving on the master path of those like Jesus and Babaji.

I think one of the things that was most helpful to me was to understand that *the Spirit is that which cannot be destroyed.* If you understand that you are One with the Spirit, then you can-not be destroyed. Most people think that they are separate from the spirit—that God is *outside* of them or "somewhere else," or that you have to die in order to be with God. This misthinking leads to death. The only thing you have to correct is your imagined separation from God! Incidentally, you cannot separate yourself from God. That is like thinking you can separate a sunbeam from the sun.

You cannot separate a sunbeam from the sun. You cannot separate yourself from God. You are a cell in God's body. You are like a piece of pie. The whole pie is God. When you, one piece, are taken out of the pie and placed on a plate, you are *still* pie! Thoughts of separation from God make you sick and make you die. Even if you do kill off your body with those kinds of thoughts, your soul cannot die. Therefore you will be left with yourself without a body, and you will have to reincarnate and try it all again. I hope you will get it this time. If you don't, at least you are sowing the seeds of mastery in your consciousness for the next time.

Three Aspects to Handling Physical Immortality

I.   Develop the *philosophy* of Physical Immortality

    A.   Get your mind and body in harmony with the Eternal Spirit.

    B.   Go to seminars on the subject.

    C.   Listen to tapes on the subject (Unraveling the Birth/Death Cycle by Leonard Orr).

    D.   Read the Immortalist literature.

II.   Develop the *psychology* of Physical Immortality: Unravel your personal Death Urge

    A.   Study your family traditions. Find out how your ancestors died and at what age. Choose not to copy them.

B.   Unless your parents are already Immortalists, you probably inherited a Death Urge. This personal Death Urge will kill you unless you kill it. You kill it by unravelling, one at a time, your negative thoughts and feelings about life.

C.   Death has no power except that which you give it in your own mind. Nobody can kill you but you. Nobody can kill you without your consent. Life is stronger than death.

III.   **Develop the** *physiology* **of Physical Immortality: Practical Mastery of the Physical Body**

A.   Study breath mastery-rebirthing.

B.   Get your body handled through the various body therapies. I recommend Rolfing and the Heller method; also Traeger and other integrative work.

C.   Master food and sleep. Reduce sleep and reduce food. Experiment with fasting. There are even Breatharians who live on the light of God and do not need food, so that blows your belief systems about food.

Quote by Leonard Orr

The biggest cause of human body death is probably the denial of or ignorance of your natural divinity, and thus the misuse of power of the human mind through negative thinking. The second biggest cause of death is probably inhibited breathing, which causes deprivation of oxygen to the blood, arteries, heart, brain, other organs and cells. The third biggest cause of body death is probably overeating, which pollutes the blood stream. Three meals per day is the secret to death, not health. Moderate fasting not only improves health and aliveness, but also seems to reverse the aging process. The predominant scientific theory of aging is excess cell pollution, which seems to be caused by overeating and underbreathing. Filling the body with plenty of oxygen and spiritual energy through conscious breathing cleans the cells.

You are already immortal until you prove otherwise: Dying is more difficult than living. (It takes a lot of effort and negative mental mass to wipe yourself out.) The following affirmation has saved thousands of people from death. I recommend that you memorize it and master it through meditation. Mastering this affirmation now is like having your own personal guardian angel to protect you. Thoughts are angels.

I AM ALIVE NOW, THEREFORE MY LIFE URGES ARE STRONGER THAN MY DEATH URGES. AS LONG AS I STRENGTHEN MY LIFE URGES AND WEAKEN MY DEATH URGES, I WILL GO ON LIVING IN INCREASING HEALTH AND YOUTHFULNESS.

(P.S. You may feel "Yes maybe I could preserve my body, but what about natural disasters, I can't stop them!" I assure you that, if there is an earthquake, and you are an Immortalist, you will not be standing where the earth cracks. If there was a plane crash and you were an Immortalist you'd survive or you wouldn't even make it to the plane that day. See Chapter 8 on Surviving the Prophesies of Doom.)

Strengthening Your Life Urge

I will close this chapter by listing ways that you can strengthen your Life Urge:

1. Take Physical Immortality seminar as much as possible. Contact the Rebirthing community and Loving Relationships Center nearest you for information.
2. Read the Immortalist literature (see Appendix I).
3. Do Aliveness Enrichment affirmations (see Sondra's book).
4. Do lots of rebirthing.
5. Join the One-Year Seminar (explain importance of chosen family).
6. Go to parties instead of funerals.
7. Give up negative, deathist friends—or enlighten them.
8. Get into the idea of Youthing. Give your body correct instructions to reverse aging.
9. Listen to tapes on this subject.
10. Goals—make up a list of:
    100 things you want to do
    100 things you want to have
    100 things you want to be

Be careful how you go out there and talk to people on the subject of physical immortality, until you are clear on it.

8

Surviving
The Prophesies of Doom

A lot of people have asked me what I thought about the prophesies—predictions of natural disasters, for example. Usually I have sidestepped the question. I did not know what to say and I did not want to think about it. I never was satisfied with the responses I tried to give, nor were those who asked me. I kept avoiding the whole thing until I was mysteriously led to three different gurus (besides mine) all of whom said the same thing. I started to pay attention, but I still was afraid to write about it. I was resisting it completely—so much so that Babaji, my teacher in the Himalayas who often teaches me in dreams, had to appear to a friend of mine and tell her to tell me to write about it. So I will. Not to do so is probably unethical.

I want it to be very clear that my intention in writing this chapter is to do all I can to prevent any kind of disasters by waking up everyone to the fact that our thoughts do affect the environment constantly. The trouble is, we take it all for granted. Most people who are not Immortalists just think they are "passing through," so they not likely to love the earth as much as if they were going to make it a home for hundreds or thousands of years. Once you start thinking about longevity and sticking around a long time, you really start loving the earth more. (At least that is my experience.)

It has been predicted that, because of the evil that has accumulated on the planet, the mass negative thinking and the group death urges, our planet must go through a major purification. By our own wickedness and folly, we are setting it up to destroy ourselves. History proves that thoughts of victimhood held by enough people can create natural and social disasters like earthquakes, floods, plagues and wars. (A mass of negative thought in a million people can easily cause an earthquake. People tired of life can cause plane crashes by their thoughts.)

In other words, many great thinkers are saying that the day of spiritual purification is upon us now!

What can we do about it?

A LOT!

The purpose of prophesies of doom is to effect change. We, the masses, can actually prevent the disasters by changing our thoughts. The purpose of natural disasters is to wake up the sleeping masses. ARE WE GOING TO WAIT UNTIL THE DISASTERS HIT BEFORE WE WAKE UP?

It is the law of nature that, if we are unwilling to discipline ourselves, the physical universe will discipline us! In any disaster only those will be destroyed who refuse to be awakened and who cling to the darkness and evil in their hearts.

DON'T YOU BE ONE OF THEM!

WHAT ARE YOU GOING TO DO ABOUT IT?

Wake up! You can begin now by upgrading your thoughts about yourself and the physical universe. If you walk about hating life, hating yourself, hating the world and hating God, you are literally contributing to world disaster. Yes, *you*.

The Hopis have been telling us for thousands of years that *our own actions* determine whether the great cycles of nature bring us prosperity or disaster. Few have listened to these enlightened beings who have never had war or famine on their land.

WHAT ARE YOUR ACTIONS?

The law of karma rules:
What you put out you get back.

You can start right now by changing all your negative thoughts. By changing your thoughts, you can change the thoughts of those around you. Become a self-appointed preacher or prophet and help others raise the quality of their thoughts.

Even if natural disasters did take place, your positive attitude and faith in God would cause you to be guided by inner direction to a safe place. Or you would allow yourself to somehow be guided by inspired psychics who would help you maintain your body, mind and spirit in safety and health.

Since thoughts are powerful, it does not pay to dwell on the prophesies of doom. Then they will become self-fulfilling, since what you think about expands (just as the nuclear leak actually happened after people went to the movie *The China Syndrome*). Also, believing in them, and especially dwelling on them, can create emotional disturbance. If you were to dwell on this kind of thing you could actually become sick, accident-prone, or create your own early death before the prediction actually happened!

Are you going to let the prophesies be *damaging and self-fulfilling* or *inspiring?* That is up to you.

The choice is Life or Death

The choice is God or Ego

What is *your* choice?

If you are choosing life and God, then you'd better wake up and purify yourself. It isn't just your conscious thoughts you have to change. ALL thoughts are creative, including your unconscious ones. In fact, those are the ones to be really concerned about. Your subconscious thoughts are producing results even though you are no longer thinking them.

You may wonder what all this has to do with birth and re-birthing. A lot! Many of the thoughts you formed at birth are destructive to you, to others and to the planet. They are being "broadcast" and are producing negative energy fields all around you. For example, some of the decisions babies make at birth (and it is now proven pre-verbal thought definitely exists) are these:

Life is hostile.
People are out to get me.
I need pain in order to survive.
Somebody is trying to kill me.
Men hurt me. Women hurt me.
I can't get what I want and I hate God.
I will get even forever for this pain.
I hate God for putting me here.
I don't want to be here if this is it.
I have to fight in order to survive.

These are common thoughts formed at birth because of the trauma involved. I am sure you can see how this affects you, your body, your relationships and ultimately the planet in every way. Now you can see why we rebirthers are so determined to help heal these suppressed thoughts and why we are so interested in new methods of birth to reduce birth trauma. (My next book will be *Ideal Birth*, part of which is about underwater-birth—the Russian method.)

If you are walking around with any of the above suppressed thoughts, or similar ones, you are going to feel a lot more miserable than necessary and the earth will not be a pleasurable place for you to be. Plus those thoughts are literally affecting the cycles of nature!

It is quite obvious: If people don't handle these suppressed thoughts sooner or later they will bring disaster upon themselves —or the pain will be so great in their bodies that they will want to "check out."

If prophesies of doom frighten us, it is only because we have victim consciousness (in other words, we feel "at the effect" of the universe or that the universe "did it to us"). This is misthinking. We do have control over our personal reality and environment. However, this cannot be done by force, effort or tension. It is done by freedom of choice over your thoughts. High thoughts that you persist in, sooner or later produce high and beautiful reality. Breathe into wonderful thoughts and exhale the bad ones.

Many spiritual leaders feel that the survivors of the purification will become immortal spiritual Masters. They say that the spiritual energy of the earth has been raising gradually over the centuries and that the human race has been making a transition from sinner consciousness to Christ Consciousness. The Bible says: "The corruptible will put on incorruptibility" and the mortals will put on immortality."

To further quote Leonards's writings:

The ordinary people who practice truth, love and simplicity, and who remember God, are not in danger. They are the spiritual government of the world. They are self-sufficient emotionally and economically. They will rebuild the world after the existing governments and evil people have been destroyed. Only to the extent that worldly governments merge with the spiritual government can they survive. The true spiritual government is invisible and eternal. Therefore enlightened people are not frightened or concerned when worldly governments and economies crumble. The righteous prosper and the wicked are cut off.

People who have pure hearts and love their neighbors will create harmony and aliveness wherever they go, no matter what is happening around them. *Be one of them.* Don't be immobilized by prophesies of doom or any disasters that do occur. Become a spiritual Master yourself.

Any time you catch yourself going into gloom over the news or events occurring around you, *STOP! Think about God instead.* Change any negative thought to a positive one. Love the Earth. The following affirmation will keep you safe.

I AM SAFE AND IMMORTAL RIGHT NOW.

Think it. Chant it. Become it.

Then if an earthquake hits, you won't be standing where the earth cracks.

9

How Personal Laws Run (And Ruin) Your Life!

After you start breathing consciously you will sooner or later get in touch with your own "personal law" (your most dominant negative consciousness factor). I would rather get you in touch with this *sooner*; since it is the culprit of your mind. So here goes. Please fill in this sentence; make sure there is a subject and a verb.

My most negative thought about myself is _____

_____

Believe me, until you get rid of that thought, life is going to be very hard for you! Your personal law is the cornerstone of the Ego (collection of negative thoughts you have about yourself). It is the one that is the major block to your happiness and aliveness. The trouble is that you are addicted to that thought. You have had it since birth or before. Perhaps you even brought it with you from a past life. Worse still, you have been trying to prove that it is right! This is how your ego has you tricked!

It is important to understand this basic principle of metaphysics: WHAT YOU BELIEVE TO BE TRUE, YOU CREATE.

This means that, if you believe your personal law about yourself (which you *did* "buy into" somewhere along the line), you will create situations to prove it is so.

For example, if your thought is "I am not good enough," you will constantly (unconsciously) set up situations that come out so you look not good enough. You will go after these situations and create them. You will come out looking and feeling not good enough, and then you will say "This proves I am not good enough." The only way out of this trap is to destroy your personal law absolutely. It may be hard at first, because you have so convinced yourself it is true. Start like this:

I forgive myself for thinking *I was not good enough.*

Since I was the thinker who thought I was not good enough, I am also the thinker who can now think **I am good enough.**

(You probably won't believe it at first, since you have indulged in the negative belief about yourself for years and years. You have to start convincing yourself of the new thought. If you don't start now, you will be stuck forever.)

There will also be resistance to giving up this thought completely. That is because your whole life has been about proving it, wrestling with it and working around it. When it goes, that will be the death of that part of your mind and your whole reality will change. Some people are so afraid of change that they would rather hang on to what is familiar and die than to leap into a new reality that would bring more life. Don't be like that. Change is fun. Sometimes we are afraid of change because our birth was a big change from liquid to air and we got hurt in the process.

But there may be fear. The fear comes because it would be *unfamiliar* to not have that thought about yourself. People are often afraid of the unfamiliar. I assure you that it will definitely not only be better without that thought, it will be Heaven compared to hanging on to it. In this case the unfamiliar you are afraid of is Heaven consciousness—and more fun than you have ever had. So relax and ask God to help you give it up. The Ego (which is an expert in confusion) will try to trick you into thinking it would be dangerous to go for Heaven Consciousness. The purpose of the Ego is to "seek love but never find it," and you will probably encounter a lot of resistance as the Ego tries to hang on to the thought and tries to prove to you that you are not of God. Don't let the Ego rule! Go for Heaven!

Two of the worst thoughts of the Ego are (1) death is inevitable and (2) your personal law (most negative thought about yourself). Both of these are just thoughts you can change. However, when the Ego is threatened, it puts up great resistance.

There may also be fear because you know that if you gave up that personal law you would have a tremendous increase in energy. This is true. If you are afraid of energy it is probably because you are afraid of God. Probably you are afraid of God because you think God kills people. This is a common mislearning from places like Sunday School, where children are taught "The Lord took him away" after someone died. I always interpreted this to mean that God would kill someone without notice and this terrified me of God. The churches and schools have been confusing the issue of death. We have been left confused on the issue of death. Until we learn the truth of what Jesus said—"The power of life and death are in the tongue" (in other words, all death is suicide, and you are the one who determines what happens to your body)—we will be afraid of God, blame God for death and hate God.

When you understand that death is the result of the thought called the Ego (the death-is-inevitable thought) and life is the result of the thought called God, you won't be afraid of God.

God brings more life. Of course then you have to love life! *Loving life is a result of loving God and loving yourself and having wonderful thoughts.* Therefore it must go like this:

> *Since I love myself and I love life and I love God, my life is going to be good. Since my life is going to be good, I am willing to have more life. Therefore I am willing to give up my most negative thought about myself, which will bring me more life. The result will be more happiness.*

The reason I am spending so much time on this point is that I have seen among the rebirthing community itself how long it took most of us to give up our personal laws completely. I noticed that until rebirthers became really clear on physical immortality they tended to hang on to their personal laws. It was almost like they were afraid that they would die letting go. This confusion cleared up and they felt safer and safer in letting go when they came to understand that their bodies were safe. This comes hand in hand with grasping the concept of physical immortality.

My own resistance was tremendous. I knew that I should work on affirmations to counteract my personal law. I wondered why I didn't. I worked on all other kinds of affirmations instead. But that negative thought kept rearing its ugly head in all areas of my life. I had a dramatic breakthrough on it one time while teaching the LRT in San Diego. It was Lent; Easter was coming. During the God section I was feeling very holy. I was wearing a white silk pantsuit with Chinese Immortality symbols woven in it. I had a lovely white gardenia in my hair. For some reason I jumped up and started shouting. Something was roaring through me. I was out of control in what I was saying, but I did not try to stop it. "This particular group must need to hear this" I remember thinking. I did not stop myself. I was shouting

"YOU HAVE TO CRUCIFY YOUR PERSONAL LAWS!"

I was very surprised that that particular word *crucify* came out of me. I figured it was because of Lent. In that second the whole audience gasped. I looked down and there was a large spot of blood on my silk pants. My wrist was bleeding. I still have the scar. I had not cut myself, I had had a stigmata! God was telling me

"YES, THIS IS IT!"

From that day on I have been "ranting and raving" around the country about personal laws.

I have mentioned this in my other books. It does not hurt you to read it again. This time I am emphasizing it more. In the Loving Relationships Training we have had to increase the time spent on clearing personal laws because it became obvious to us that it was one of the most important things to be done. What if, for example, you had a personal law that went like this: "Nothing works for me." Then even the affirmations we give you wouldn't work! Nothing would work until you ultimately changed that thought.

So I beg you, for your own sake, do not take this chapter lightly or pass over it as if it were not so much. WAKE UP! Allow the Holy Spirit to undo this thought that has been wrecking your life.

With every breathing session, the personal law is more exposed and "loosened." I suggest that you consciously breathe in the new affirmation (for example, I AM GOOD ENOUGH, or whatever the opposite of your negative thought is). This new thought should be your personal mantra. You will need to meditate on it, think it always, chant it, write it and look at it on the wall. Remember the old thought may have been in there thirty to forty years, or even lifetimes. I rebirthed myself for five solid hours on this one issue in the presence of Leonard Orr on the Hopi reservation that Easter Sunday. Your results will tell you how you are doing. Results are your guru.

Incidentally, I feel it is very important you know your mate's personal law and your business partner's personal law.

10

How Your Birth Affects Your Relationships

Most people wonder why, when they love each other so much, their relationship soon gets stuck and becomes difficult or even impossible. One of the main reasons is that

LOVE BRINGS UP ANYTHING UNLIKE ITSELF

This means that when someone loves you, the energy of that love penetrates you and pushes out of you, like a master cleanser, whatever is suppressed (i.e., fear, anger, guilt and negative thoughts). *Your* love is doing the same thing to your mate. Therefore while this "stuff" is coming out the relationship can get very strained and strange. The Loving Relationships Training and other seminars mentioned are designed to help you learn how to deal with that.

One of the things that occurs is that the thoughts you had at birth will be pushed up and out of you. Some of these thoughts could be:

> Men hurt me.
> I can't trust men or women.
> People hurt me.
> Life is hell.

I have to be angry in order to survive.
I can't get out.
I have to get out of here.
Nobody wants me.

Thoughts like these, PLUS your particular personal laws based on your particular birth trauma, will begin to surface. If you don't know about this, the relationship can get very crazy. Remember, these thoughts create results continually, which are often projected onto the partner. If a woman has a thought "Men hurt me" that she formed when the obstetrician smacked her bottom when she was born, she will then be putting out that thought psychically in the form of a command:

MEN! HURT ME!

She will be psychically demanding this from her man. She could set him up to hurt her to prove she is right. Partners unconsciously act out the negative psychic thoughts (demands) of their mates out of love. This is because love takes upon itself your negative so you can see it more clearly. A mate will literally act out the negative thoughts of a partner in order to heal him or her, usually without realizing it.

What is really going on in most relationships is that BIRTH TRAUMAS ARE COLLIDING. Besides that, family patterns are dovetailing. With all this going on, it is no wonder we have such a high divorce rate. I think it is hard to manage a relationship well when you do not know anything about your partners birth script or his or her personal laws. This is one of the main reasons I created the Loving Relationships Training and my book *Loving Relationships.*

Another thing related to birth that often comes up in relationships is the feeling of No-Exit Terror. "I have to get out of here." When the intimacy is high and the love is intense, the energy usually stimulates memories of being crowded in the womb and being trapped. This feeling is then projected onto the relationship. Acutal fear of suffocation could come up and cause a partner to leave suddenly for no apparent reason.

There may be unnecessary fear of pleasure in a relationship because of birth memories. The bliss of the womb was followed by something painful and fearful. A baby can get the thought "pleasure is followed by pain." Therefore, when the relationship gets too pleasurable, a tremendous fear can follow, causing a person to withdraw, leave, or stop the pleasure because of fear that pain will follow.

There is often a basic fear of letting go with another person, or a fear of touching, that is not noticed during the courting stages of a relationship. After the couple begins living together and earlier intimate family and birth memories are activated, a person could start feeling unsafe about letting go and/or being touched because at birth that person was mishandled and became afraid. I am saying that, the more that person feels loved, the more the fear might come up—again because love brings up anything unlike itself and anything that was suppressed.

In the beginning of the relationship most of these birth memories are suppressed. An example is extreme separation anxiety. A partner might be terrified of being left by a mate, or even of being left alone. This again may not have been noticed in the courtship. We can often trace these fears back to the moment the newborn infant was suddenly taken away from the mother to a nursery where it felt totally abandoned. I have had clients cry for three hours straight while re-experiencing that moment of separation from the mother.

There could be sex-identity problems related to birth that will affect a relationship. Perhaps the parents wanted a boy and got a girl. This girl may grow up feeling she is never good enough as a woman and she may end up always feeling inferior to her husband. He may get tired of this low self-esteem and want her to leave. She may feel she has to leave anyway before she becomes an emotional cripple.

Fear of sex may show up (since sex leads to pregnancy and pregnancy leads to birth and birth leads to memories of one's birth trauma). All of this could be just too much to deal with, so the easy way out could be to make sure that sex can't happen.

I have been discussing ordinary births. Complicated births are another thing. Cesarian babies usually grow up with an "interruption pattern." This could affect relationships, because the person may not be able to complete things. Breech babies often grow up with a terror of hurting people. They may unconsciously do it anyway, because that is how they survived in the first place.

Lack of breastfeeding can also affect a relationship. Some of these babies grow up feeling undernourished and never feel satisfied no matter what their mates do—because their basic thought is "I can't get enough."

What goes on in the womb definitely affects relationships. I refer you to the brilliant research of Dr. Thomas Verny, who wrote *The Secret Life of the Unborn.*

I think you may be getting the idea that your birth script definitely could be affecting your relationships! Incidentally, if you have read my other books and some of this chapter is repetitive, it certainly won't hurt you to be reviewing it.

I recommend that you are patient with yourself and loving about all this. There is time. Pieces of your birth material may come up for years. You will let it up a little at a time, which will be safe for you. If you have a partner who is open to self-improvement and as willing to purify his or her mind as you (obviously you are or you wouldn't be reading this book), then you are fortunate indeed. What you can do is make a game out of clearing these factors and assist each other on the path to healing them. It can be a healthy, exciting part of your relationship. We rebirthers have done this in our relationships. We have always been, quite honestly, relieved to have insights into these matters, rather than to be *stuck* with situations we did not understand.

If your relationship gets stuck a lot, it is because some negative thoughts need to be cleared. Getting rebirthed ASAP is the best first aid I know of. Of course, I highly recommend the Loving Relationships Training, where you will be taught how to clear relationships quickly.

I have always felt that anger is hard to deal with and produces fear and shutdown in relationships. Some of the most difficult cases I have ever worked with were people who had a birth script that led them to be very angry (at the doctor for forcing anesthesia on them, using forceps or inducing labor, etc.). They were very angry at birth and they survived, so their particular script turned out to be "I need anger in order to survive." It was very hard for them to give up anger because the way they had it set up was that if they gave up anger they would die. This kind of complex wiring from birth can be very hard on a relationship. And again, I am sure you can see the extreme importance of making births gentle and without trauma. I venture to say that those people who had easier births had easier relationships. Again, we cannot blame the doctors totally. We all created our own birth script based on our past-life karma.

The main point is this: be thankful that we know how to erase birth traumas and negative personal laws. It is easier to correct than it is to stuff it, suppress it, wrestle with it and pretend it is not there. Again, all it is is thoughts—and you can change thoughts. I always say, *bliss is just a thought away.*

You can even get to the point where nothing bothers you. Your mate can be going through something and you have a choice. Either you let it bother you or you don't let it bother you.

I recommend "more fun per hour" myself. This I learned from Bobby Birdsall.

11

Other Spiritual Practices and Rebirthing

I do believe one should try everything that works. Rebirthing does not take away from any other discipline or religion. It only adds clarity to it.

Meditation and Rebirthing

I recommend both. Meditation gets you nicely centered. I do not see a conflict in doing both techniques. They enhance each other! I have noticed, however, that some of my clients who have meditated for many years before coming to Rebirthing are incredibly powerful as a result. However, sometimes all that power going behind their birth thoughts. Personal laws and the thought "Death is inevitable" has made them more stuck in those thoughts. Thus Rebirthing was a tremendous relief as it helped them let go of some thoughts that had not surfaced in meditation because they were meditating alone. I personally love a combination of both Rebirthing and Meditating.

Chanting

Evoking the Divine Presence in this way is wonderful and exciting in the body. To me it burns out the ego and karma. I do not see any conflict between Rebirthing and Chanting. I love both. Babaji taught me that *Om Namaha Shivai* is the highest thought in the universe. Chanting it gets one very high. It means:

Infinite Spirit/Infinite Intelligence/Infinite Manifestation

Therefore things manifest more quickly when one chants. This mantra also means:

I bow to Shiva, the part of God that destroys ignorance.

Therefore by chanting you are "burning out" negative, ignorant thoughts as in Rebirthing. Practicing both Chanting and Rebirthing is really dynamite.

Prayer

One of the greatest things I could ever do for you would be to get you to read the *Course in Miracles*. I share with you here a prayer method that, when done daily, will endlessly enrich your life. This is most pleasurable when done aloud with a friend, a lover, family members or a small group.

Daily Prayer

1. *Opening:*   Read aloud at least three pages from the *Course In Miracles: Text.*

2. *Gratitude:*   State out loud those things you are grateful for today.

3. *Forgiveness:*   State out loud the things you want to be forgiven for and those people and things you want to forgive

                     and/or

   State what you want to be released from.

4. *Petition:*   Ask God for the things you need and want and the changes you want to see in yourself.

5. *Closing:*   Read aloud a lesson from the *Course In Miracles Workbook*, and commit yourself to recalling it throughout the day.

This daily prayer ritual works without fail. Just try it for one week and you will see what I mean. If you continue it for 365 days, you will be just *amazed*, I assure you!

Become Awake!

Become Spiritually Nourished

Every Day, Have A Spiritual Practice— A Form Of Worship And Prayer

Meditate

Chant

Rebirth

Pray

Sing

Do Affirmations

Love God

Take Action

Participate

12

Rebirthing and Healing The Body

Having been a nurse, with a Master's degree and fourteen years of experience in many areas of nursing and medicine, I feel I am capable of speaking out on the subject of healing. I actually learned more about healing, however, after I left medicine and began studying metaphysics. I can unequivocally say that I have never seen anything heal a body like Rebirthing or Conscious Breathing.

I quit nursing one day as I was passing out pills for the hundredth time and I realized that those pills were no guarantee at all that my patients would be healed. How did I know that, after they stopped the pills and went home, the illness would not come back? I didn't know. I realized we were nowhere in medicine until we understood what caused the disease in the first place. I felt that I was on the wrong end of medicine. I was trying to heal people *after* they had the disease. I realized I should be *preventing* people from getting sick and going in the hospital. This would be my new mission.

I felt totally committed to it. The chief of our department was very sad. He said "Why do all the good nurses quit?" He was almost in tears. I had been good. It was my first year in a hospital after my two-year experience in the Peace Corps. Nobody had ever died in my presence. That was important to me. I told him I had to quit. Later I tried other areas of nursing, and I ended up being a prenatal nurse. I felt I was most productive teaching new mothers how to have healthier babies. But it never felt really right.

In 1974, when Leonard tried out Rebirthing on me, I became absolutely fascinated by the effects of birth trauma on the body and by how one's thoughts affect the body. When Leonard convinced me that all pain was the effort involved in clinging to a negative thought, and that negative thoughts could be changed and breathed out, I knew for sure this was it. I immediately gave up medicine altogether in order to study this new thing.

One day I approached Leonard in the hall and asked "How do I become a rebirther?" His answer was simple: "Handle your own birth trauma." I went to the basement immediately and began having wet rebirths as often as I could take it. We had not even discovered dry rebirthing at the time and everything was dramatic for us as pioneers. The two years I spent with Leonard and the gang doing research on the birth trauma and its effects (and subsequently developing rebirthing into what it is today) were two of the most fulfilling years of my life. It became my passion, my mission, my constant research, and my life. I never had seen anything that produced permanent healings before my very eyes, in myself and others. I myself had had a pain in my body for the fifteen years since my father died. I had tried everything in medicine and psychiatry, but nothing worked. When this pain disappeared completely forever after three or four rebirths, I was "sold" forever!

The history and development of Rebirthing (which I think is exciting) is in the book *Rebirthing in the New Age*. When you read that you will have a new appreciation of the process. We are still in the first decade of Rebirthing and still learning from it.

Of course it is perfectly fine to get help from the medical profession. You should honor your fears if you still fear you cannot heal yourself. It may take you awhile to learn self-healing. Rebirthing is a good place to start. Once you understand that your thoughts produce your results and that your body is "at the effect of" (responds to) your mind, you will then understand the *Course in Miracles* when it says *"The physician is the mind of the patient himself."*

When I was a nurse I used to wonder why people got sick. I interviewed a lot of my patients about what had gone on in their lives right before their body broke down. It was usually an emotional upset related to a relationship breaking down, a traumatic incident, or the death of a loved one. I became so amazed at how much illness was related to problems in relationships that I began searching for an answer to relationships; the Loving Relationships Training is the result of that research.

However, when I was a nurse I still was not clear how the mind caused disease. I had not learned enough metaphysics to put it together, although I did have an awareness that most disease was psychosomatic. Once I became clear and enlightened enough to understand that THOUGHT CREATES RESULTS and that THE MIND RULES THE BODY, I was able to understand what the *Course in Miracles* means when it says "All illness is mental illness." Once you accept this, you can heal yourself. If you will just "get" that you created your symptoms and disease yourself with your mind, then you will get that you can uncreate it with your mind. Quite simply, once you locate the negative thoughts that created your symptoms/disease, all you have to do is change those thoughts to positive ones. Now, this takes a little commitment on your part. Changing a thought *once* that you have had for thirty years is not enough. The new affirmation must be repeated over and over until your mind is reprogrammed. (See my book *I Deserve Love* for detailed explanations).

The conscious raising of your thoughts to higher thoughts and Conscious Breathing (breathing in the new thought and breathing out the old thought) can produce permanent healing. I have seen people in Rebirthing heal themselves of cancer—tumors being reduced, and so on. I have known deaf people to start hearing after rebirthing. It is very common now to see these "miracles," and I do not talk about them much as they are so ordinary to me. In my presence people often heal themselves faster because of my certainty that anything can be healed and that anything created can be un-created. (I, for example, healed my own baldness after wearing wigs for two years!)

Even after understanding how the mind itself creates disease, I began to wonder why in one patient the liver was affected, in another ulcers resulted, and in yet another skin eruptions occurred. Why, if it was all due to the mind and nerves, were different parts of the body affected? Why in my case did hair loss occur instead of ulcers? These questions haunted me. I was fortunate to have in one LRT a great metaphysician-healer, Louise L. Hay, who did this research herself. I was very relieved when she gave me her wonderful little book *Heal Your Body: Metaphysical Causations for Physical Illness.* I highly recommend you have several copies of this little book. They are nice to give to friends and to people you meet while traveling. Here, with her permission, are some of the discoveries made by Louise L. Hay.

Metaphysical Causations for Physical Illness*

Problem	Probable Cause	New Thought Pattern
Allergies	Who are you allergic to? False ego & sensitivity.	I am at peace. The world is safe & friendly.
Back Problems	Lack of support. UPPER; lack of emotional support, holding back love. LOWER; lack of financial support. Fear of money.	Life itself supports me. I trust the universe. I freely give love and trust.
Colds	Confusion, dis-order, small hurts. Family and calendar beliefs.	I am a free thinker. I am at peace in my own mind.
Diabetes	Deep sense of sorrow. No sweetness to life.	I allow life to be FUN. I let the past be just that. I accept joy & fun as the basis of my life.
Eye Problems	Not liking what you see in your own life. Fear of the future. Not seeing Truth.	I see with loving eyes. I like what I see, I see clearly, I see the Truth.
Fatigue	Resistance, boredom. Lack of love for what one does.	I am enthusiastic about life, & filled with energy.
Gas Pains	Gripping undigested ideas. Gulping air from fear.	I relax & let life flow through me with ease.
Headaches	Tension, emotional upsets, hurt feelings. Uncertainty, fear.	Peace, love, joy, relaxation. In my world all is well.
Itching	Unsatisfied desires, remorse. Punishment for guilt.	Whatever I need will always be here. I accept my good without guilt.
Jaundice	Prejudice. Discolored beliefs.	I feel tolerance & compassion & love for all people.
Knee Problems	Inflexibility, fear. Ego, pride, inability to bend. Stubborn.	Forgiveness, tolerance, compassion. I move forward without hesitation.
Lung Problems	Afraid to take in and give out life.	The breath of life flows easily through me.

*Copyright © 1976, 1979 by Louise L. Hay. Used by permission.

Mouth Problems	The incapacity to take in ideas. Set opinions, closed mind.	I welcome new ideas & new concepts.
Nerves Nervousness	Communication. Struggle, rushing, fear, anxiety. Confused thinking.	I am on an endless journey through eternity. Peace, be still. There is nowhere to rush.
Overweight	Insecurity, self-rejection. Seeking love. Protecting the body. Trying to fulfill the self. Fear of loss. Stuffing feelings.	I accept & love myself as I am. I am always secure in spiritual nourishment. I allow myself to feel.
Pain	Congestion, blockage. Belief in bondage. Punishment for guilt.	I release any need for punishment. I let go & let life flow through me.
Rheumatism	Lack of love. Resentment. Chronic bitterness, revenge.	I have compassion for others & for myself. I accept joyful feelings.
Stomach Problems	Incapacity to assimilate ideas. Fear of new ideas.	I assimilate new ideas easily. Life agrees with me.
Throat Problems	The avenue of expression. Repressed anger. Emotional hurt swallowed.	I freely express myself with joy. No one can hurt me, I am at peace.
Ulcers	Something eating away at you. Anxiety, fear, tension. Belief in pressure.	Nothing can irritate me. I am peaceful, calm and at ease.
Veneral Disease	Sexual guilt. Belief that the genitals are sinful or dirty. Need for punishment.	I lovingly & joyously accept my sexuality & its expression. There is no guilt & no punishment.
Warts	Belief in ugliness. Guilt, hate for the self.	I do advertise ugly thoughts. There is NO guilt. I love all of my body.

This is only a partial list of metaphysical causes for physical illness discovered by Louise L. Hay. Copies of the booklet *Heal Your Body* may be ordered by sending $2.50 for each one (tax and postage are included) to Louise L. Hay, 1242 Berkeley, Santa Monica, CA 90404; or order by phone at (213) 473-9253.

My "Ultimate Truth Process" for Self-Healing

Any time you have any negative symptom in your body, be it as minor as a headache or a disease as serious as cancer, you can begin clearing it immediately in the following manner. Take out three sheets of paper and write at the top:

1. The reasons I have this condition are:

   _____

   _____

   _____

   _____

   Keep writing all the reasons until they begin to repeat themselves. They will come out as negative thoughts. Some of them may sound ridiculous. Put them down anyway.

2. My "payoffs" for having this condition are:

   _____

   _____

   _____

   A payoff is a negative, "neurotic" reinforcement of something you are getting to prove. What do I get to prove by having this condition?

3. My fears of giving up this condition are:

   _____

   _____

   _____

   _____

   You may not think you are afraid of giving it up. If you weren't, you would have already let go of it. You are probably just afraid of the new energy you would have without it.

After doing this Ultimate Truth Process, write down your most negative thought about yourself.

My most negative thought about myself is:

_____

This thought plus the other negative thoughts you have written down in the exercise are causing your condition or disease. Now simply invert those thoughts to affirmations and work with them daily. Then it is best to call your rebirther to breathe out these negative thoughts permanently from your body. These negative thoughts have actually created what we call "negative mental mass," which is causing your symptoms. The symptoms can be healed rapidly through change of thought, breathing and praying.

The main reason I do not want to give up this condition is:

_____

_____

_____ .

Now write your new Affirmations from the exercise.

_____ .

_____ .

_____ .

_____ .

_____ .

_____ .

My Spiritual Healing Course

On the following pages I would like to share a summary of a Spiritual Healing Course that I teach. Some of this information I learned from *A Course in Miracles.* Some of it I learned from my many spiritual teachers. Some of it I learned from being a nurse. Some of it I learned from my research as a Rebirther and watching thousands be healed in that way. Some of it I channelled from Infinite Intelligence. I am putting this in outline form to make you more conscious while reading it. Read each line slowly and absorb it the best you can. Review this section of the book often, meditating on what it means. If you get this part, you can save a fortune in doctor's bills and you will feel the way you always wanted to feel.

I.   **You will be healed when you see no more value in pain.**

    A.   You have to be willing to give up the "payoffs."

    B.   Sickness is a *decision*—an election—*you chose it.*

    C.   The *Course* says all illness is mental illness; the mind is "off."

    D.   The *Course* says it is that you are "trying to kill God."

    E.   Healing is a threat because it means you would have to be responsible for your thoughts. (Man even chooses death to try to prove that he has power over God!)

    F.   You will be healed when you recognize that there is no value in sickness.
       1.   Say: "There is no gain in this."
       2.   The mind makes the decision to be sick.
       3.   You did this by indulging in a negative thought (Ego).

II.   **The physician is the mind of the patient himself.**

    A.   The outcome is what the patient decides himself.

    B.   Special agents (pills, etc.) give form to patients' desires. They are not actually needed at all (*Course in Miracles*).

C.   The mind rules the body. Say "I have no need for this!"

D.   Most people believe that sickness has chosen them. This is insane.

E.   Sickness is not an accident. It is an insane device for self-deception. It's purpose is to hide reality—to keep you from seeing what you need to see.
1.   You can't heal it permanently until you take responsibility for creating it . . .
but
2.   You may resist doing this. *There is a tendency to attack what doesn't satisfy you to avoid seeing that you created it.* This is a trick of your Ego. You have to catch yourself.

III. **Pain**

A.   All pain is the effort involved in clinging to a negative thought. (Ego).

B.   In pain, God is denied and fear is triumphing.
1.   Pain is sleep.
2.   Pain is Ego (fear).
3.   Pain is wrong perspective—proof of self-deception, a sign that illusions are reigning in your mind.
4.   It is your thoughts alone that cause you pain. Nothing external can hurt you and no one but yourself affects you.

C.   Pain=fear=denying love=using pain to prove that God is dead.

D.   The body can act wrongly only when it is responding to wrong thoughts. The body cannot create (this is a fundamental error people have).

1. Believing that the body "did it to you" is a lie.
2. All material means that you accept as remedies are reinstatements of the illusions. Medications are forms of "spells" (*Course in Miracles*).

IV.   Fear of healing

A.   Sudden healing could produce depression in people who have chosen sickness as a way of life and a major way of getting attention.

B.   Do not pray for a miracle healing overnight (of cancer, for example). You probably could not accept it because it would change your reality so quickly that it would produce a lot of fear.

C.   The Holy Spirit will never add to your fear.

D.   Pray for removal of the *fear* of healing first.
   1.   The idea here is that every time you give up something negative, you get more energy and more awareness of God. Ths is what we are really afraid of.
   2.   Misery pain, conflict and death we are all "used to" and "addicted to." We are addicted to the Ego. It is familiar.
   3.   What we are really afraid of is the unfamiliar: Peace, more life, more God, more love and more energy.
   4.   So we tend to hang on to a condition (sickness, pain, or a problem) that brings us down because of fear of more energy (God). We do this because we are so confused that we think God kills people, so we'd better not have more God (energy). Ths keeps us stuck!

5. You have to get clear on God and Immortality first.

E. You have to stop pretending that sickness and pain were "accidents." You have to stop pretending that you did not make them up.

1. You saw an imagined threat (illusion) which you made real, and then you made up a defense (sickness, symptoms and pain), then you pretended you *didn't* do it and that it is all beyond your control.

2. Then you will be *mad* at God because you feel lousy. Again, you will attack what does not satisfy you to avoid seeing that you created it (*Course in Miracles*).

3. You have to stop this insanity and see that it is a useless game. It is a plan to defeat what cannot even be attacked (life and God and immortality).

4. The whole useless game keeps the mind split.

5. Even killing yourself to get out of pain is no solution. Death is no solution. Consciousness, when departing from the body, automatically seeks its own level. (In *The Door of Everything*, see the chapter on Physical Immortality.)

6. You may hate God because you are sick or in pain, but I assure you the reason you are sick or in pain is because you hate God.

F. Rebirthing is a simple, wonderful way of healing yourself. Since Rebirthing, which is conscious breathing, is pulling in the spirit on the inhale, and releasing the ego (negative thoughts) on the exhale, you can literally pump out all thoughts that made you sick!

V.   Healing will flash across an *open* mind.

    A.   All healing is temporary until you heal death.

        1.   Don't say: "Well I don't want to live forever because I feel too lousy, or because I am in pain, or because life is hell."

        2.   Get that: The reason you feel lousy, have pain, have sickness, etc., is because you bought into the idea of death in the first place. You are already what Jesus described as "the walking dead."

        3.   As long as you still think "death is inevitable" you will have to create some sickness to prove you are right.

    B.   The *Course* says "Death is the result of the *thought* called the Ego. Life is the result of the thought called God." Are you going to choose the Ego and try to kill God? It won't work. Death is no solution. The soul lives on and does not go to a higher level if you kill off your body. Death is an illusion. You are still stuck with yourself. There is no escape from your own consciousness.

    C.   When you stop placing limits on the body, its health will be restored and it will no longer be affected by weather, fatigue or food.

    D.   Study the book *The Door of Everything* very carefully.

VI.   The Atonement heals with certainty.

    A.   Say: "I am one with God and I allow the Holy Spirit to undo all my wrong thinking." (This is the Atonement.)

B. The Atonement cures all sickness.

C. The Atonement takes away the guilt that makes sickness.

D. The cure must come from holiness. God abides in holy temples.
   1. If you "get" that there is no place that God is not, then there is no place that sickness can be.
   2. Where you are sick is where you are still into the Ego.
   3. Where you are sick is where you are still denying God.

E. Only Salvation can be said to cure.

F. The sole responsibility you have to produce miracles is to accept the Atonement for yourself.

G. All healing is essentially the release from fear (Ego). The *Course* says there are only two true emotions:

   Love   or   Fear
   (God)   (Ego)

H. The Ego is a collection of negative thoughts you have about yourself. To be healed completely they have to be undone.

I. Healing and wholeness:
   1. To heal is to make happy. You have had many opportunities to gladden yourself and you have refused them.
   2. All forms of sickness (and death) are physical expressions of the fear you have of *Awakening*. They are attempts to reinforce sleeping. Sleep is withdrawing—a form of death. Death is unconsciousness.

3. Healing is release from fear of *waking*. All healing involves waking up and replacing fear with love.

4. If you are sick, you are withdrawing from God! You are spiritually deprived!

Closing Comments on Healing

There is a spirit in man, and the Inspiration of the Almighty giveth him understanding," says Job. This spirit in man is his God. The Inspiration is his breath of God. The God within and the God without are united by breathing. But the external breath of air into the lungs is only a symbol, a hint of the true breath which right thoughts can give, if they are put forth and taken in at the moment of intense experience. It is equally powerful if in a moment of great joy one keeps firmly to the same great TRUTH. Firmness is poise, balance of character. This is a great healing quality. We become healers of disease according to our poise of character. (Emma Curtis Hopkins, *Scientific Christian Mental Practice*, p. 82).

Here is the affirmation that has ultimately enabled me to heal anything in my body:

*I allow the Holy Spirit to undo all my
wrong thinking that has created this condition
and that keeps me from giving it up.*

Write it. Say it. Say it to your rebirther and breathe! Tell God you mean it!

13

Rebirth Experiences

Phyllis

I, Phyllis, now choose life.

This is one of the new conclusions I have drawn from a very powerful rebirth I just experienced with Sondra. As I told the Truth during my rebirth, some incredibly complex "wiring" in my subconscious mind revealed itself to me. I share this with you in the hopes that it will bring you and your clients to a deeper level of insight and healing.

Apparently, out of love for my mother and out of my experience of observing how she acted and of communicating with her, I somehow linked holding my breath and survival: "In order to survive, I must hold my breath." If I breathed, she wouldn't like me and I would die. In addition, I discovered I had it wired up that if I let go completely, God would kill me. And the final crazy piece of wiring that revealed itself was that I also had "aliveness equals death."

I experienced painful paralysis of the hands during the rebirth and was terrified of letting go, because letting go also meant

God would kill me. I did continuous affirmations to counteract these beliefs:

> I am safe and Immortal right now.
> The more I breathe, the more I live.
> The more I breathe, the more people love me.
> The more I let go, the more God loves me.
> God is safe.
> God supports life.
> God is life.

I still had difficulty letting go, and then Sondra acknowledged me for managing to live so long and do so well while having such a powerful belief system that supported death. We both laughed and my hands started to loosen up and the energy started to flow more freely through me. It was a miraculous experience. I have been an avid seeker of God for ten years now and all I can say is: It's a good thing I didn't find Him until I changed the belief from "God is death" to **"God is life."**

Rex

My very first rebirth was really an experiment to see if there was any value in the process for me. It became an astounding visual experience. My rebirther directed me to breathe deeply and talk about everything I was feeling. Like a Panavision movie, I imagined myself standing on a pyramid in the desert watching storm clouds moving away into the distance. All at once I saw a large ball of yellow light hovering near the desert next to the pyramid. It was enormous in size and extremely powerful in aspect, reminiscent of the atomic bomb explosions we all saw in the movies years ago. I was fascinated with it and couldn't take my eyes off it. Suddenly, I realized that the ball of yellow light was me, my essence, my soul, the real person inside. I was awestruck by the energy and power of what I saw, and also aware of how little of that energy and love showed through me into the world I lived in. If I were able to draw on that much life force, my life would have been very different, more dynamic, more dramatic and more fulfilling. How could I ever hope to tap more into this gigantic life source and become a fuller expression of myself? My rebirther suggested that I continue the rebirthing process, and I readily agreed. The possibilities had been revealed to me.

Wendy McL.

My most powerful rebirth was my first one. I had done some yoga, but nothing had prepared me for the totally altered state of this simple breathing process. I began breathing slowly and gradually felt my body fill with energy. Within a short while I felt tingles in my arms, legs and face; it seemed as if a golden cast of energy were surrounding me and I was floating on it. I reassured myself that I could wiggle my toes and fingers if I tried. As I relaxed into the energy my breath began to change. It felt very cool and blue in color and I began to feel that the breath was breathing me. Then I reached a state where I did not breathe and felt totally connected to my spiritual self; I had a sense of myself as spiritual on a level I had never known before. My breath began again, and I felt that I followed rather than directed it. I felt very high and peaceful and awestruck. It was my fantasy of what a good LSD trip would be. I came out of the rebirth feeling relaxed, refreshed and shocked by the experience. Later that night I got angry at something, expressed it and felt so clear it was as though I could see sky inside myself. It was an experience of what it would be like if we let go of our feelings rather than stuffing them or hanging onto them. I was unable to even think about or discuss the rebirth with anyone until shortly before the next session because of how profoundly it changed the way I saw everything.

Lori

My first rebirth was so impressive to me that it convinced me immediately of the power of rebirthing.

I was at a seminar and had never been rebirthed. During the course of some processes (which seemed quite innocuous) I started crying and becoming very emotional. The seminar leader told me to take a few breaths and lie down and relax. Before I knew what was happening I began to tingle all over; there was to be a rebirth later in the day, but since the process had not yet been explained I knew absolutely nothing about it.

I started to feel paralyzed and I didn't know what was going on. I really trusted and felt safe with who I was with, so I kept going. I was really fascinated with what was going on in my body. In the past I had been able to express emotions, but doing the connected breath while crying really changed the complexion. I noticed I wasn't thinking the way I usually did and felt liberated from my mind for the first time in years. I had quite a long rebirth although time became irrelevant. When I started coming out of it my first thought was "I don't want to think again." I was in a daze for a long time, but at that moment I knew that what had just happened had, and would continue to, change my life.

Tommy

After my first two rebirths, I got into a hot tub just to relax. I started doing some connected breathing and immediately went into hyperventilating. I wasn't sure what was happening, but felt safe enough to relax and surrender. The whole process continued for about three hours and I experienced a lot of tetany. There was a terrific amount of energy pouring out of my arms and hands.

Toward the end of it all, I was feeling high enough to ascend right then and there. I then experienced a vision of Jesus surrounded by a warm golden light. I'm not sure how long it lasted; he just seemed to be affirming my presence. I remember dreaming of performing miracles someday, and laughing at the thought of my walking on water and then crying at the thought of it actually happening.

There was a lake beside the hot tub and I then walked down there to cool off. I didn't go right in the water, but sat on the bank just letting it all sink in. And then without thinking, I ran to the water with my arms outstretched toward the heavens. I hit the water running and I KNOW my first two steps were actually on top of the water. It was an amazing experience that only took a few seconds and when I realized what had happened my feet sank to the bottom. I've only told a few people about it because of fear of ridicule. But I know it happened and it changed my life.

Love, truth and simplicity.

Wendy C.

My best experience of rebirthing was on my seventh or eighth rebirth with Geri. I was feeling upset about something I can't recall at all. I was very insecure about my body. My jaws didn't even fit together right—my teeth wouldn't mesh. I talked for awhile with Geri, then started breathing. I remember having lots of different images in my head that didn't seem to make any sense. At some point I realized I had come out of it. I just stretched my body out. I felt so relaxed and so at peace. Then I closed my mouth and noticed my teeth fit again. I had an intense feeling that I knew exactly what I was doing, that everything was going correctly.

Richard

My best rebirth was as part of a group rebirth at the advanced LRT. It was the first time I experienced pre-birth thoughts. Essentially, what I realized was how angry I was at my parents even before my birth—especially my mother. My anger was based upon the belief that my mother was trying to prove something to her parents by having a child; trying to validate herself through me. What really sent me for a loop was realizing that that is what I most dislike about myself (looking outside myself to validate my experience). No wonder my personal law was "I'm not good enough"—I could never get validated enough "out there." Going through experiencing the anger, then the personal guilt and coming out OK was a tremendously releasing experience and something I am grateful for.

Doreen

This experience was later on in my rebirthing. I had lost count of my rebirths by this time and most of the drama was gone. As

I lay down to breathe that day I could feel some tightness in my body. I had been feeling somewhat overwhelmed by all the work I needed to do and I could feel the old struggle thoughts begin to emerge. I was tired, I had been working hard again and my body needed a rest.

I started to breathe in the presence of Jane, my rebirther at the time. I was well able to feel her love and support as usual. I could feel some sadness in my chest area for all the time I had struggled. I kept breathing at an easy steady pace. I began to gently cry easing the tightness out and the more I cried, the more my body began to relax and surrender to the energy within it.

At that moment I could feel my heart open to its fullest, something I had never felt before. And a rush of joy and gratitude moved through me. I continued to cry this time, it was not from sadness but from gratitude. My breathing changed again. It felt rhymically connected to what seemed to be the sea. All the images I had worked on in meditation were no longer images, I actually felt like a wave on the sea. I could feel this light energy fill my body, glowing like a child's night light. I could feel God's presence fill the room surrounding the bed which seemed to gently rise up off the floor rocking both Jane and myself.

At that moment Jane softly whispered "Oh, my God" and shared the same experience I was feeling. The bed was glowing with white light pouring from the center of my heart chakra. And all I could do was cry with joy. I felt helplessly connected to God as though he had reached deep into my being and touched my very core and essence. I knew that God had revealed himself to me in a way I had never experienced before. And since, I have never questioned what happiness is.

14

The Art and
The Science of Rebirthing
by Bob Mandel,
Certified Rebirther

Rebirthing is a process of surrender.

The purpose of rebirthing is to surrender to the healing force of your own aliveness, and to do so with a maximum of ease and pleasure and a minimum of struggle and resistance.

Rebirthing is a highly personal experience. Generalizations about the process can be taken as signposts that you are headed in the right direction, but should by no means be seen as objectives to be struggled towards.

The art of rebirthing is about surrendering to and trusting your own intuition—opening your heart to your divine creative energy.

The science of rebirthing is about techniques that have proven to support this surrender.

The art is about letting go, releasing control, getting your mind out of the way.

The science is about adjusting your breath, correcting your thoughts and changing your misperceptions.

One is the feeling part.

One is the thinking part.

Both are valuable. Rebirthing is most effective when the two are in balance.

Your spiritual integrity is a function of your commitment to your own transformation as a vehicle for healing others.

In rebirthing others, the trap is: You project your own case on others as long as you are incomplete with yourself. Completion consists of the alignment of mind, body and spirit. Integration of mind, body, spirit consists of:

1. Quality thoughts
2. Physical well-being
3. Trusting God

or

1. Thinking big
2. Safety and pleasure in your body
3. Love in your heart

Physical Immortality is the thought to purify your mind and body of all resistance to Eternal Spirit.

Fear of death is fear of letting go.

Fear of life is fear of taking in.

The breath is the mirror of how we exchange ourselves with life.

In a completely surrendered circle of breath lies a person who is safe with life.

You can "read" a person's breath like his palm or foot or eyes; but the breath is more than a way to see a person; it is quite literally the vehicle between the visible and invisible world (i.e. the physical and spiritual) and, as such, it is the core of a person's being.

Your breath is your life! Rebirthing your breath is renewing your life!

Integrity from the mind is about keeping your word, or agreements, for fear of disapproval and/or guilt.

Integrity from the heart is about trusting that what's good for you serves all, and that your commitment to your own growth, combined with your compassion for others, is the most valuable service you can offer.

In Rebirthing be aware of investment in results—the "Obstetrician Syndrome"—which is control and inhibits surrender. The solution is not necessarily doing nothing, though that can be a valuable process, because you can be doing nothing and still "expect" miracles, which will take you out of present time and create struggle.

What to do! What to say!
1. Before rebirthing anyone, prepare yourself: Take time to clear your mind, relax, have a vision of a successful session, but invite the Holy Spirit to *do* the rebirthing. You are the witness, the guide—not totally detached, however. Compassion leads to telepathy, but too much sympathy leads to struggle.
2. Getting started
   a. verbal clearing
   b. breath check
3. In the middle
   a. breath adjustment
   b. affirmations when appropriate
   c. personal law work
   d. "I love you," the most healing words in the universe.
4. Completion
   a. grounding
   b. homework
   c. next appointment

Rebirthing is letting go of what is not.
Rebirthing is letting it out, not figuring it out.
Rebirthing is creative science of rejuvenation through breath.

15

What It Was Like to Write This Book

I became "pregnant" with this book Christmas Day, 1981. I was on my way to Campbell Hot Springs to visit Leonard and discuss the revision of *Rebirthing In The New Age*. Somewhere between Reno and Sierraville, while meditating in the back seat of Mark's car, I became very clear that I could not rework that book. A new book was coming in. I realized that it was already "overdue." I told Leonard it was time for a new book and that was it. He agreed.

I had, however, tremendous resistance to getting at it for some reason. January passed, February was going and March was approaching. One night in my hotel room in Marin, where I had just taught an LRT, my business consultant practically got down on his knees begging me to go to Hawaii to settle a business matter there. I said "Okay." (Why should I resist going to Hawaii?) It still did not occur to me to do the book. I thought I was going to Hawaii on a business trip.

Three days before I left for Hawaii I got a call from my friend Abbe, very early in the morning. She had had a dream. In the dream there were floods, earthquakes and mudslides. People were dazed. I was in the dream. I was fine. The Babaji, my guru, appeared and told Abbe to tell me to get busy and write a book and explain to people why this was happening. I had tremendous resistance to the dream. I knew what it meant but I did not want to think about it. I had had so much resistance to the "prophesies" that Babaji did not even try to get through to me in dreams as he usually does. He had to appear to my friend instead. It was then I knew I was going to Hawaii to write a book.

In meditation, the only place I could get that I was supposed to be for writing this book was with my friends Robert and Loy Young, two immortal Masters who had just returned from the mystic schools of Tibet. I recalled visiting their "Esoteric Research Foundation" on my last trip to the islands while they were away in the Himalayas. I recalled that they lived in a beautiful original plantation-style house in Pacific Heights. I remembered the place being fixed up like a temple. It was very pure and holy and I had felt very saint-like there during the brief time I had spent receiving some body work. I called Loy and told her that I must be with her. She said "You come right ahead."

The day I left I felt high as a kite. I had just done four exquisite rebirths. On the plane I wrote about twenty-five love letters. When David Tassaka picked me up at the airport, I was soaring. I was thrilled to feel the energy of the islands penetrating me. We stopped at McDonald's for an ice cream. My mind was racing. Two books were coming in my head at once! It was astonishing to me.

To my surprise I suddenly went into complete resistance and shut down. I had a sudden sharp pain in the brain and felt "blinded." At that *second*, mind you, my billfold "dematerialized." It was absolutely nowhere to be found! Twenty minutes after arriving on the islands I had lost all my money and all my ID. The only other time this had happened was twenty minutes after I left Babaji's ashram the first time in India. I went through a major identity change then. Here it was again. I let go. I was going through a major identity change again. There was nothing left to do except get busy and do it. I certainly could not waste time shopping! I went to the beach. That night I looked in the mirror and I looked different. Something was happening.

Loy and I had breakfast together on the terrace overlooking Honolulu. We spoke of spiritual matters and our work. I soon forgot about my billfold, as I felt so blessed to be in her presence again. I shared some papaya and then told her I had to go on a fast. She showed me to my sanctuary. It was Monte's room, she said, but he would not mind as he was gone for a few days. Everyone at the Foundation was so gracious to me. I had fresh juices brought to me, and beautiful gardenias and Hawaiian flowers were put on my writing desk and altar every day.

I still had tremendous resistance. Nevertheless, I kept writing. The only break I took was for a morning dream workshop that Loy was teaching. The name of it was "Dreams are the Doorway to God." When I walked into the room, to my amazement, she was saying "Sometimes when the Masters are trying to give you a dream and you are resisting it, they will appear to a friend who will be told to pass the dream onto you." I had not even told her of that dream my friend Abbe had.

My resistance continued. Every day I fasted, chanted and meditated. All of that helped. However, the resistance continued in some form or another until I got to the chapter on prophesies. As soon as I began that chapter my typewriter went crazy. It began to make very strange noises and part of the frame literally jumped off the key board! Robert actually had to come and repair it. After I finished the chapter, I felt healed. The fourth day I had already finished most of the book!

The fifth day I moved down to the beach with my friend Roger Lane, who first produced the Loving Relationships Training for me in the Islands. The breezes from the beach soothed me. The singing birds enchanted me and the plumeria blossoms put me in ecstasy. Every day I went to the beach for two hours and listened to my chanting tapes with stereo earphones. I seemed to be more and more in bliss. On March 3, I "delivered" a long overdue baby, this book. Roger and Jackie, our friend from New Zealand, and I went out to celebrate it at a Thai Restaurant called Keyo's. We had wonderful spring rolls placed on lettuce with cucumbers and mint leaves topped with a sauce made out of sweet vinegar, shredded carrot and roasted chopped peanuts.

That night the rebirthing energy was so strong in Roger's house that everyone who walked in the door went into a rebirth. I was up late rebirthing them. It seemed that the manuscript, which was lying on the table, was already doing its work.

The next day I had the whole manuscript blessed by a Kahuna, who kept it in her lap for twenty minutes. (Thank you, Morna, I love you.)

For Information

1. Telephone 800-641-4645, extension 232.
2. Rebirth International
    c/o Rima Beth Star
    1000 Jausting Place
    Austin, Texas 78746
    (512) 327-7809
3. The LRT National Office
    c/o Bob Mandel
    145 West 87th Street
    New York, NY 10024
    (212) 799-7323 or 7324

16

Poetry by
Vincent Newlin, Rebirther

I AM
  A POET
    OF LOVE
&
    IMMORTALITY.
MY WORDS
  ARE FREE
    AND PULSING—
THE WORLDS
  LOVE ME
  AS I RISE
WITH PASSIONATE FREEDOM
    &
    DELIGHTFUL
    AIRS
      OF LOVE.

I

Something inside of me
has reached to the place
where the whole world
is breathing.

Hymns and songs
of Immortality
and the great soft clouds
in God's lungs...

New air to the imagination
stirs these wings — this dove body.
I know the ecstatic light
strikes my crystal body
as I breathe.

Think on this a moment!
Our first connection is always air...
What else is it
we float about in?

This plain air wraps
a luminous being,
blissful about everything...
and always breathing...
Let your next inhale
remind you of this.

II

Music of daily influence
keynotes at your chest —
and sometimes a musical band
tightens around the ribs.

The world harmony sometimes
snares too loudly and your inner rhythm
gets tucked under.

As you draw in your daily power
and your daily song — how much
of it merely fills you up
and what share do you participate in.

There is a consideration in all this,
and it is this:
Whenever you feel your head
starting to take off like a rock,
or crashing heavy with frustration —

give a nod to that tiny sigh
inside of you
and it will grow at least an inch.

III

Old people come and go,
still no one approving —
these ancient ones of a long survival.

You know,
the youthing seeds sits inside them,
awaiting water.

You who unleash the sprinkle
of your kindness
revives the dove in their bodies,
and once more,

their feet soften
as they walk.

IV

A longer day reaches for me —
why else this blazing connection?
Today, even the yolk lays
Breathing in its egg.

Toward an affectionate tomorrow
Pleasantly I stir.
My gift for you —
a world that constantly
Returns.

V

From AND JESUS BREATHED

And Jesus wept
For the spirit moved in Him
to feel deeply the aliveness
That is in all living things.

He saw in the masses
the way people thought about things.
He saw that
they did not know
the direction of their thoughts.

The feelings of those
long sufferers gave Him
renewed strength and courage
to teach how each thought
creates life or death
according to the thinker.

And Jesus let out a deep compassionate sigh
and felt at peace.

VI

VERSIONS
OF ME

Mine is the face
of Michelangelo.

Within my heart
smiling Jesus opens for you
His bloody breast.

My hands cry the harp
that flushes
tears of God.

I sit in the Immaculate
Moments of Moments.

Miracles take their turns
performing me.

When my Breath
begins to heave its tremendous sigh
in gift of you,

touch your glowing finger
to the thinnest of my thoughts

and ride the satin wave
of satisfying Beauty.

(Thank you, Vincent, I love you.)

From the *Essene Gospel of Peace, Book Two*, I leave you with wonderful food for thought. The weary had come by the bed of the stream to seek out Jesus. "Tell us, Master, how may we talk with the angels and stay within their holy circle?" And Jesus spoke to them. He talked about the Ancient Communions. "The first communion is with the Angel of Sun," he said. "The second is with the Angel of Water..."

> The third communion is with
> The Angel of Air,
> Who spreads the perfume
> Of sweet-smelling fields,
> Of spring grass after rain,
> Of the opening buds of the
> Rose of Sharon.
> WE WORSHIP THE HOLY BREATH
> Which is placed higher
> Than all the other things created.
> For, lo, the eternal and sovereign
> Luminous space,
> Where rule the unnumbered stars,
> Is the air we breathe in
> And the air we breathe out.
> And in the moment betwixt the breathing in
> And the breathing out
> Is hidden all the mysteries
> Of the Infinite Garden.
> Angel of Air,
> Holy messenger of the Earthly Mother,
> Enter deep within me,
> As the swallow plummets from the sky
> That I may know the secrets of the wind
> And the music of the stars.

Epilogue
Let The Reader Be Aware

Reading this book has probably been unlike any book reading you have done before.

Putting this book down and returning to life-as-usual may be easier said than done.

If you surrendered to the experience that the words of this book invite you to feel, your breathing, and your life, may be in the process of permanent change, and you may want to avail yourself of some suggestions to support and facilitate this transformation.

Signs of change:

If your body is tingling,

If you feel light-headed,

If your body temperature is changing a lot,

If you can't stop breathing,

If your chest is tight,

If your feelings are changing fast and furiously,

If you're having infantile physical symptoms (rashes, etc.)

If you're remembering things you haven't thought of for
years or never even knew you knew,

If you're having weird thoughts such as "I don't belong,"
"I can't make it," "It hurts to be alive,"

If you're feeling unjustifiably separate, sensitive, scared
    or shy,
If you don't seem the same to yourself,
the chances are you're in the midst of a spontaneous rebirth.

Don't Be Alarmed! You're Just Waking Up.

Spontaneous rebirths are as old and as common as mankind.
Whenever you are overcome by awe, beauty, love; whenever
your limited sense of yourself is challenged by an undeniable
experience of a larger presence in your life that your mind cannot
comprehend and your heart cannot resist, you are rebirthing:
surrendering and connecting to a Source that is safe, powerful
and replenishing, but because it is unfamiliar to you, you fear it
at first. As a child learning to swim, the water is unknown and
known at the same time. It can happen on a mountain top or in a
cave, on a desert or at sea, running in a marathon or gazing at a
leaf. And it can easily result from reading this book.

What To Do
If You Are So Overcome By This Book
That You Don't Know What To Do!

1.   Relax. Breathe easy. You are safe no matter what you
      think. Whatever comes up is on its way out and you
      never let more up than you are ready to let go of. What
      has happened is simple: The tremendous amount of love
      and aliveness put into these pages has activated your
      resistance and fear for the purpose of release. Trust the
      process.

2. Surround yourself with supportive people. There are communities of people all over the planet supporting one another in releasing the resistance to breathing fully and freely which, after all, is just the fear of life itself. Take a breath into greater safety.

3. Get rebirthed by a certified or registered rebirther. Rebirthing is such a profound simple process that some people foolishly fall into rebirthing themselves as a substitute for getting rebirthed, thinking they'll save time or money. Make no mistake about it: there is nothing like ten good sessions with a fully qualified rebirther, someone who has cleared away enough of his own personal "stuff" to create the space for you to do the same, easily and pleasurably. You can avoid a lot of struggle and/or self-delusion by rebirthing with a professional.

4. Don't rebirth others before you are properly trained. If you get rebirthed and feel a passion for rebirthing others, you can be trained by high-quality rebirth trainers to be a professional rebirther. It is an exciting career where you can make a contribution to the well-being of others as you support your own growth.

5. How successful you are as a rebirther will be determined largely by your spiritual integrity, i.e. your commitment to your own evolution and your willingness to take complete responsibility for your creations.

6. You should know that in committing yourself to rebirthing, you are expressing the desire to open yourself to more love in your life and that to feel your commitment to love is not only to heal yourself of the affects of birth and perhaps conception, but also to heal your relationships at their origin with your parents and family.

7. Rebirthing can open the door to experiencing your purpose in being here—the reasons you chose your parents

and they you. To feel these original choices is to forgive your family completely. To feel the perfection of your whole life is to forgive God completely.

8. Rebirthing is the celebration of love and life; and the dance of breath is the divine reminder of why we chose to play on this planet in the first place. Life can finally fulfill its promise of being a heavenly reward instead of a hellish punishment.

What an awakening!

What a universe to be part of!

Take a deep breath...Let go...

In releasing this book you are inhaling into the greatest journey of your life.

Bob Mandel

Appendix I:
Especially For Rebirthers

Love Letter to Rebirthers

I love you! Again, thank you for your work in the world and your devotion to Rebirthing. I'd like to talk with you about how we can improve our work and ourselves, how we can clear up Rebirthing at large, and how we can do further important research. I am also sharing my new basic interview form with you.

As we all know, what makes a good rebirther is: Love of God, Love of Life, Love of Self, Love of Others and Love of Rebirthing itself. Of course, clarity and intuition are the keys. If we are clear, our intuition is accurate and we instinctively know what to do, what not to do, what to say, and how to "be" in a rebirth. If our own "case" is in the way, our natural intuition is blocked and we may contaminate a rebirth. Not only is it important to be able to "put our own case aside" during a rebirth, it is also important to realize God is doing "it" through us and we need to get "out of the way."

As a rebirther, knowing how to process oneself by oneself is absolutely essential. I hope that the LRT helps everyone learn how to do that faster. Knowing how to rebirth oneself and knowing when it is necessary is extremely important. There can be a danger of thinking we are clear when we may not be. There can be a danger in thinking we don't need any more professional trainings. The biggest mistake, perhaps, is thinking we do not need to be rebirthed frequently ourselves. To stay ethical with ourselves and our work, we should get rebirthed by another qualified rebirther at least two times a month. (I got this answer by interviewing five female rebirthers who told me they knew they needed at least that much by other rebirthers in order to stay really clear.) This can be worked out as a paid arrangement or a simple trade agreement. I think we should make it standard ethical practice. Rebirthing is always more effective with another there because you go deeper and can't avoid something as easily.   .

Rebirthing is an art *and* a science and I feel we need continual practical training in all areas of Rebirthing. Just to keep up on the latest research is reason enough. I think we should become as professional as possible, while maintaining the uniqueness of our understanding of surrender and lack of form. Instead of just leaving it all to intuition, I think we should take trainings and surrender to each other's teachings. The ego is tricky. We may need to be cleared up just when we think we don't. Checks and balances are important. Leonard made up the Certification Game in order to help maintain the quality of Rebirthing. It is also the best game I know to master your own case. I have found it immensely valuable to throw myself at the feet of other trainers who would nail me on my case and not be willing to put up with my escape mechanisms. So why not go for affiliation? It may not be necessary, but to me it is still the best game in town to heal one's case fast. It is not required, it is optional, but I hope something I say inspires you to want it. To me it has never been a game of ranks or a power trip. I used it to clear myself. It worked. For that reason I was elected a leader. That is because I have been willing to have my ego smashed. It is worth it. The short amount of agony that one might go through getting processed by a colleague in public is nothing compared to the long-term agony of "dragging it out" and wrestling with it for years.

Make it easy on yourself! Let other trainers help process your case by participating at the highest level you can. And remember all differences are temporary, as *there is no time.* If it takes you longer to get certified than someone else, SO WHAT? Maybe your labor and delivery took longer.

I just want to say that when I did not let myself surrender to other trainers and I tried to do it all alone, I ended up in trouble with a lawsuit. I couldn't even keep my own ego "in check." I will not make the mistake again of not looking at myself carefully through the eyes of others. If we are really "hot" as rebirthers, we shouldn't have to remind ourselves that we may need to be processed or rebirthed. (It is very clear and spontaneous to know we need our cases handled, need to be rebirthed by another, or need to take more training.) One way you know for sure is by your results!! Are your clients getting stuck? As a group, all of us must be willing to continue taking trainings from each other and learning. There IS a network of continuous deep training you can receive. There are ten-day programs, ten-week programs and six-month programs. If you have never taken a rebirth training longer than one or two week-ends, I would have to say this is inadequate, and unfair to your clients and you. A long-term program gets you down to the nitty gritty in relationships. In summary, I would have to say that if you are a rebirther who has had very little professional training from other qualified rebirthing teachers, I ask you

Are you in ethics with yourself and the Universe?

If you are not, sooner or later you will punish yourself and I am trying to spare you that.

As a group all of us must be willing to continue taking trainings from each other, and especially from good teachers. I love taking trainings from LRT trainers and Rebirthing teachers to learn about all their latest research and keep myself clear. It is exciting!! Last year I took two LRTs as a student and trainings from both Diane and Fred, plus of course Babaji, the community itself, and other Certified Rebirthers. This is going on all the time and I recommend you take advantage of it. I ask you as a group please to encourage other rebirthers to upgrade their training and increase the number of times they are getting rebirthed by another rebirther (besides one's mate). If we find a rebirther who resists doing this, we should handle their resistance. If we see another rebirther being inappropriate (unethical about sex and rebirthing, for example), we should handle their case and/or report it to Rebirth International.

We are all responsible for the quality of Rebirthing in the Whole World. The more Rebirthing is respected, the healthier and happier our lives and practices will be. (The happier our clients will be and the happier we will be, and the better the world will be). I am sure you know all this or you would not be rebirthers. I am merely reminding you. Let's all remember the importance of our commitment to Rebirthing at large in the world.

To maintain the quality of Rebirthing, I recommend the following:

1. **Continue your personal training.**

   I have already covered the importance of this. It is easy to find out what trainings are being given in your area if you are active in the Rebirthing Community. It is fun, easier, and more productive to be actively involved in your Rebirthing community. If there is no community action going, create it. Have weekly meetings of rebirthers even if you have to start them yourself. This is much better than trying to do it "all on your own." Let yourself be supported. You may have to clear some resistance to "family" in order to be in the rebirthing and LRT family. The way to clear up one's own case with ones original family is to surrender to the immortal family. The spiritual family.

2. **Continue your own self-rebirthing.**

   Hopefully you have completed your rebirthing process to the point that you have had a breath release and have learned to safely rebirth yourself. (If you doubt or question whether you've completed your breath release, you probably have not.) I recommend rebirthing yourself frequently. However this does not substitute for the need to be rebirthed by another rebirther. Breathing a little every day is a good idea, but if I were you, I would give myself one good long rebirth or more every week. I always travel with a snorkel and noseplug as if it were now one of my standard toiletries. There is no reason to be miserable. Jump in the tub and rebirth yourself. If you are not comfortable with this you need more wet rebirthing training. When your head is down there under water and you want to come up, breathe past that for a little while and find out what is on the other side of that resistance. Ask someone to come in the bathroom and sit near the tub if you feel unsafe alone or if you have trouble disciplining yourself to go for it.

3. **Continue to get rebirthed by another qualified rebirther— at least twice a month.**
   This is the important thing. I have already explained why. Everyone should also have a confidant, in my opinion, other than a mate. If your mate rebirths you, that is better than nothing, but still not as ethical as if you actually go surrender to another professional rebirther. This will take pressure off your relationship. Another danger of having just your mate rebirth you is that you could be distracted, end up making love instead, confuse your transference too much and generally be less focused. It is a common danger when two rebirthers live together. So I am talking about another qualified rebirther besides your mate. I strongly recommend you get rebirthed in both hot and cold water.

4. **Staying in the Immortal Family.**
   I have not found anything more valuable (besides rebirthing itself) than surrendering to the family. From the family you will receive support, clearing, feedback, and release

from old family habits. Staying in integrity with a whole group is the real challenge. You may fool one or two friends or colleagues, but fooling a whole spiritual family is almost impossible. You may be shy or embarrassed or prefer to hide rather than let the whole family see you falling apart. However, falling apart is approved of in our families. We know the ego has to fall apart for the true divine self to emerge. Anyway, why try to hide your case? It will only "get you" later. Surrender!

I often have to laugh when rebirthers compete for clients in a city of eight million people. Surely this is ridiculous and can only be a symptom of sibling rivalry patterns. Support each other. Find out how much fun it is to help each other with clientele and developing a business. Listen to the tape Phil and I did on "Rebirthing as a Business." Get off it about competition.

Competition is free advertising!

5. **Observe what kind of clients you have attracted and what that says about your own case.**
    Do you have five clients in a row who can't let go? Do you have six who can't pay you? Your clients will teach you everything. Pay attention. Appreciate them. What are they telling you about you?

6. **Belong to Rebirth International.**
    If you do not like the system, be part of changing it until you do. We are always changing everything. Nothing is static. I remember when Peter Kane had the nerve to mail all the Certs his complaints about the way we were doing things. His letter was brilliant. We listened to him. We adopted many of his ideas, put him in charge of Committees and made him one of the Directors. He deserved it. We want your contributions to change. We want you in this family. Go for affiliation. For you, if nothing else.

7. **Start teaching seminars.**

We teach what we need to learn. It is a fast way to learn. I remember when I was stuck with only five students at a seminar. That is all I felt I could handle. I kept creating five students only. Then one day I got safe enough to teach ten, and later fifteen. I had to go up by increments of five. Then one day I remembered there is only one mind and I allowed more. A teacher has to learn twice as fast as his students and has to be able to learn from his students. You are a student and teacher at the same time. To teach something well, you will want to master it. We need more good teachers.

8. **Master the Physical Immortality seminar.**

What I really hate to hear about is that someone began rebirthing without the knowledge of Physical Immortality having been given to them by their rebirther, nor had they heard about it in any seminar. I do not feel this is appropriate at all! It could even be dangerous. Rebirthing someone without teaching them physical immortality is inappropriate because with every rebirth they become more powerful. If they have power behind the thought "Death Is Inevitable" they could kill themselves faster. One of the most important things Leonard ever taught me is that it was unethical to teach enlightenment without studying death. Because you could end up using all the power of enlightenment to kill yourself faster, if you did not understand that death comes from the thought "Death Is Inevitable"; and that the thought could be changed and one could be an Immortalist in the Physical body if one wanted to. Not to be clear on this is not to be a good rebirther. People must know from you that they have a choice about death. You as a rebirthee must understand the line in the *Course In Miracles* that says "Death is a result of the thought called the Ego. Life is a result of the thought called God." Of course the thought of the ego that produces death is "Death is Inevitable." You as a rebirther must understand how rebirthing goes hand in hand with the option of Physical Immortality and, ultimately, the ability to dematerialize and rematerialize. If you do not fully understand this connection, then I feel you are ripping off your clients and yourself. I recommend you review all physical immortality seminars available. Physical Immortality leads to developing the ability to have all possiblities available, including dematerializing and rematerializing. Some clients may not be ready to completely integrate that, but it is important that you yourself as a rebirther are coming from the point of view that in the space of God, there are no limitations and all things are possible. No limiting thoughts. This consciousness will dematerialize the stuckness. And, make no mistake, the results in your clients are a result of your own clarity combined with their karma and level of enlightenment. You, as a rebirther, I hope and pray, want to provide for them the highest level of consciousness possible. (love, safety and certainty). If your life urge is clear, they will have phenomenal results and you will be serving God with LIFE ITSELF... which is God. *If your own death urge is in the way, where are you, really, as a rebirther?*

Meditate on the pursuit of EXCELLENCE in your work. If you have trouble getting clear on this, take Fred's seminar on the pursuit of excellence.

9. **Take the Loving Relationships Training.**

    I do not say this just because I created it. I just assume you want to be a good rebirther and you love being good at what you are doing. I assume that you know that a good rebirth depends on the *relationship* between you and the rebirthee. Therefore the way to be a rebirther is, I think, to understand the "dynamic" of relationships thoroughly. The LRT is a result of all my research as a rebirther, with special emphasis on how one's birth affects relationships. The trainers have recently rewritten the LRT for the twelfth time, agreeing on each point, which I feel is a major accomplishment! The more knowledge you have of how birth affects relationships, the better rebirther you will be. And, of course, your own relationships case will get cleared up. Therefore, why not take the LRT? If you have resistance, I would like to hear about it, because all of us as rebirthers need help on our relationships, and so do most people. It is an integral part of our work, and I welcome your research on the subject.

10. **Read all the literature available on the subject of rebirthing and immortality.**

If you have not read this available information I feel you are ripping yourself off (in processing your own case, for example) and ripping off your clients. I feel this is one of the standard ethical things a rebirther of any standing will do naturally. I recommend the following books for study to improve your work:

a. *Rebirthing in the New Age* (Orr and Ray)

This book has been cleaned up, updated, and given a new cover. Although this was a bit "dramatic," rather "California," and a bit off in places, the general information was excellent and still is. It does give a fair and truthful account of how it was to be a pioneer in Rebirthing. Those are the facts. I am not embarassed too much about our beginnings. The point is, there is a lot of incredibly valuable information in that book on Rebirthing. It is available to you so that you can become an expert. Yes, rebirthing has evolved—that is why I have written a new book—but I stand behind the original as a teaching too. Master those principles. That is my advice. Become as good as you can become. That is my advice.

b. *Celebration of Breath* (Ray)
This book I acknowledge you for reading. Please spread the word and get other rebirthers up-to-date about it. I hope your clients like it also. It is for people new to rebirthing, old-timers and rebirthers themselves.

c. *Rebirthing: The Science of Enjoying All of Your Life* (Laut and Leonard)
This is a new book by Phil Laut and Jim Leonard. I have not read the whole thing but I was involved in a debate on certain pages, and I know I can recommend it.

d. *Birth Without Violence* (LeBoyer)
This should be basic reading material for every re-birther, and it is important to have new clients read to you aloud from this book, especially starting at "This is the Golden Age" until the end of that chapter. Assigning this to all clients makes your work easier and helps them move faster.

e. *The Secret Life of the Unborn Child* (Verny)
This is what rebirthers have been waiting for. Study this with gratitude. We have been waiting for this research on prenatal psychology. Assign this to your rebirthees without hesitation.

f. Books on Immortality
Master these:
Rebirthing in the New Age (Chapter on Immortality)
The Door of Everything (Chapter 11)
The Life and Teachings of the Masters
Physical Immortality (Leonard Orr)
Psychological Immortality
etc.

g. Get grounded in *A Course in Miracles*.

11. **Look at your commitment to Rebirthing.**
    It should be your passion and your lifework.
    Are you willing to be on call twenty-four hours a day?
12. **I hope you will take the God Training I am creating in Bali.**

This year I have been especially studying prenatal psychology and our work, and I would appreciate your cooperation on focusing more on the prenatal period. We do extensive work on this in The Advanced LRT if you would like more experience on how to work in this area. I am also studying the personal law, how tricky it is, and especially how the personal law itself could keep you from healing your personal law. Say a client has a personal law "I am a failure." Then he might become a failure at healing his personal law! Please note the tricky aspect of hanging on to one's case. Remember the ego has a big investment in NOT getting off it.

Another thing I feel we need to handle is clients' fears of letting go or giving up their case. We should study how one's particular birth script affects the way one might let go of the case: easily, resistantly, fast or slow? For example, somebody who couldn't wait to get out of the womb will perhaps be eager to get off it, whereas an induced birthee may have to be *induced* to get off his induction numbers. In other words, your birth experience probably makes you resist or not be able to do the behavior that would heal it. Study this carefully in your own case. Keep me informed so I can write about this. Also remember that, since one's birth script produced survival, a client may feel like this: "Since I was angry at birth and I survived, the way to keep surviving is to stay angry." Therefore even though their anger may be slowly killing them, clients will think they might die if they give it up, based on their birth script. We, as rebirthers, must give them safety affirmations: I can survive without my anger; the more I give up my anger, the more alive I am; etc.

I have the strong feeling that the better your first interview with a new client, the better everything will be down the road. So I have written for you my idea of the ideal interview. You can order these forms from the LRT office. I welcome your additions and corrections.

Finally, I hope you will carefully study the work of Jim Leonard and Dr. Eve Jones.

In gratitude and love,
Sondra

The LRT
Rebirthing Interview Form

Rebirther should interview client by asking questions instead of having client fill out form in order to make it more personal and to establish relationship.

1. Name of client   Sex
2. Where were you born? State   Country
   In what facility? ☐ Hospital   ☐ Home ☐ Other
   What time of year?
3. Were you: ☐ Wanted?   ☐ Planned?   ☐ By both parents?
   If not, why not?
4. Do you have any siblings?   ☐ Older   ☐ Younger
   Which child were you? (birth order)
5. Were there any miscarriages or fetal deaths before you? If so, explain.
6. What did your parents or others tell you about your pregnancy?
   Any complications?
7. Do you know anything about the labor?
8. Was your birth itself normal?
   Other: ☐ Twin?
              ☐ Premature?
              ☐ Late?
              ☐ Forceps?
              ☐ Anesthesia?
              ☐ Breech? (Rear first, footling, face presentation?)
              ☐ Turned manually while in utero?
              ☐ Cord around neck?
              ☐ Placenta Previa?

- ☐ Cesarian?
- ☐ Induced?
- ☐ RH Factor blue baby? Blood exchange? Jaundice?
- ☐ Deformities?
- ☐ Dry Birth?
- ☐ Other comments?

9. Did your mother have any specific problem at your birth?
   - ☐ Hemmorrhage?
   - ☐ Infection?
   - ☐ Other?
   - ☐ Post partum depression?

10. Was your father present at the birth? Was he in the hospital area? If not, where was he?

11. Did your parents want a boy or girl?

12. Were you breastfed? If no, why not?

13. How did your older siblings feel about your arrival?

14. Any other comments about your conception, pregnancy, birth?

15. Did you have any illnesses during your infancy? If yes, explain.
   Did you have any illness in later childhood?

16. Did you have any accidents or injuries as a child?

17. Did you have any major emotional traumas as a child?

18. Were there any deaths in your family while you were growing up? If so, who?

19. Did you parents divorce? If so, what age?

20. How would you describe yourself as a child?

21. Describe your mother (beginning with what you did not like about her):

22. Describe your father (beginning with what you did not like about him):

23. How would you describe their relationship while you were growing up?

24. Any important comments about any other substitute parent, step-parent, grandparent or people who took care of you?

25. Are you now married?   Living with someone?
Describe your mate:
Any significant problem?   Sex Problem?
What is the state of your relationship?

26. For Females:
How many times have you been pregnant?
How many deliveries?
Any problem with those births or children?

27. Are you having any problem with your body now, or recently? If so, describe.
History of illness:
Any major tensions, pains or symptoms?
Are you on any drugs? What for?

28. What are your major fears, if any?

29. Are you presently under (or have you recently been under) psychiatric care?

30. What seminars and trainings have you done?

31. WHAT IS YOUR MOST NEGATIVE THOUGHT ABOUT YOURSELF?

32. WHAT IS YOUR MOST NEGATIVE THOUGHT ABOUT LIFE?

33. WHAT IS YOUR MOST NEGATIVE THOUGHT ABOUT RELATIONSHIPS?

34. Do you have any negative thoughts about breathing?

35. What have you heard about Rebirthing?

36. Do you have any questions about Rebirthing?

37. Do you understand the concepts of Thought is Creative and Physical Immortality?

38. Are you clear about the price and number of sessions, etc.?

39. Do you have anything to clear with me, your rebirther?

Form to Be Used During Rebirthing and Post Rebirthing

1. Describe client's mood before the session.

2. Describe client's breathing patterns during the session.

3. Describe any significant points of the session.

4. Other comments (general description of the rebirth):

5. Affirmations given:

6. Any assignments given:

7. Recommended readings:

8. Recommended trainings:

9. Date of next session:

Form for Subsequent Rebirths

1. Review client's original birth history.

2. Review most recent rebirthing.

3. Review affirmations given at last rebirthing.

4. Discuss results, feelings, or problems in life since last rebirthing.

Prerequisites for Rebirthers

For Affiliation

1. To have completed at least one week of Rebirth training and/or an appropriate apprenticeship program of 30 hours or more.
2. To have the intention to Rebirth others.
3. To have a willingness to continue being Rebirthed to completion and to participate as a trainee in Rebirth trainings.
4. To have certainty of your ability to produce results with the people you Rebirth.
5. To have the written sponsorship of at least one Registered or Certified Rebirther.
6. To have been Rebirthed at least once by your sponsor.
7. To present documentation of your work to your sponsor.
8. To have been Rebirthed ten times by the same **Rebirth International®** Rebirther.

Note: Annual dues are $50.

For Registration

1. To have integrated all of the prerequisites of an Affiliated Rebirther.
2. To be fully trained in approved programs, icluding completion of at least 100 hours of training with one or more Certified Rebirthers.

3. To present documentation of your work to a Certified Rebirther.
4. To have the written sponsorship of at least one Certified Rebirther.
5. To have been Rebirthed at least once by your sponsor.
6. To successfully Rebirth yourself in both warm and cold water.
7. To have assisted in at least one Rebirth training and to continue to attend and assist in trainings.
8. To have Rebirthed at least three clients 10 times each.
9. To have the ability to produce results with your clients:
   a. Completion
   b. Release of body tensions
   c. Integration of breath, ease and pleasure into one's life.
10. To assist in making support groups available for all your clients.
11. To lead successful Rebirth, Post-Rebirth, Spiritual Psychology and Physical Immortality seminars.
12. To have completed or presently be a member of a One-Year Seminar.
13. To have mastered the self-analysis principle.
14. To create successful affirmations.
15. To have motivation other than money.
16. To have trust in your intuition.
17. To have the ability to function without outside approval from your colleagues for your well-being and feeling of success.
18. To have respect and to value the divinity of yourself, your clients and your colleagues.
19. To have the ability to remain confident and competent while experiencing helplessness or weakness in yourself.
20. To believe in God and in yourself. To love and feel at home and safe in your body. To be willing to surrender to the highest thought.

21. To have the ability to function successfully in our spiritual community.
22. To be willing to continue evolving and training as a Rebirther.
23. To be willing to support other qualified members of **Rebirth International**®.
24. To be a member in good standing with **Rebirth International**®, and to maintain open, up-to-date lines of communication with your sponsor.

Note: Annual dues are $100.

For Certification

1. To have fulfilled all of the requirements for Registered Rebirther: To be a fully qualified Rebirther.
2. To have demonstrated leadership ability in supporting and evolving your local Rebirthing community for a period of two years.
3. To be responsible for staying current with Rebirthing developments.
4. To present documentation of the above at a Certification Training.
5. To successfully complete a Certification Training and the procedures of that training which means you are a Certified Rebirther (i.e., receiving a majority vote).
6. To be a member in good standing with **Rebirth International**®, and to maintain open, up-to-date lines of communications with other Certified Rebirthers.
7. To have the signature of one Certified Rebirther to serve as a witness that you have completed the above requirements.

Note: Annual dues are $100.

A Few Thoughts for Rebirthers*

Peter Kane

The main thing I want Rebirthers to know is that Rebirthing is both an art and a science; it has a form. Within every form there is a general purpose or direction and some basic techniques are used to accomplish this. In other words, Rebirthing has a pragmatic side. For example, it is a specific way of breating and we have basic ways of teaching this. It is important to acknowledge this, not to avoid it, as it is part of the science of Rebirthing. *And* the most important part of the science is using your intuition to apply it:

1. To appropriately interact with your client.
2. To direct them enough, but not too much.
3. To provide a presence of love neither smothering nor vacant.
4. To guide them intuitively in their breathing and in their psychological and spiritual transformation.

You are lovingly, intuitively, artfully and scientifically giving what you have to share about Rebirthing. It is OK for Rebirthing to be about all of this—breathing is. Being with people as a Rebirther is a great gift. Celebrate it!

---

*Peter Kane has done a lot of good research on the types of breathing one sees as a rebirther and how it relates to the kind of birth clients had, and to their death urge. For example: "The exhale represents the way people let go, the way they relax, the way they live. Pushing on the exhale is a basic death urge. It is pushing love away. A kind of 'I can't wait to get this over with' type thing. The true rebirthing breath is the opposite of all one's negative stuff about death. The full, relaxed inhale without any emphasis on the exhale purges death form the body. It becomes the biological manifestation of physical immortality."

Rebirthing Integration —
The Inside Story*

Jim Leonard

Integration is the purpose of rebirthing. A simple definition of integration is: *The process by which you cause something unknown and unpleasant to become a blissful part of your normal awareness.* Integration ultimately results in all parts of you enthusiastically supporting your aliveness, effectiveness and pleasure.

This chapter is based on the two years of research into the exact nature of rebirthing integration that I have done since I returned from visiting Herakhan Baba in India in 1979.

What causes integration? If a person does connected breathing for forty-five minutes and then suddenly integrates, does that mean it took forty-five minutes of breathing to cause that integration? My research says not. Something was present, along with the breathing, during that moment of integration, which was not present before. Had that particular something been present after one minute of breathing, integration would have happened then.

The advantage of integrating sooner instead of later is not only that more can be accomplished in each session (it can) but also, especially, that it makes the rebirthing much pleasanter for the person who is being rebirthed. Rebirthing can be extremely pleasurable if you integrate quickly, but if you have to spend an hour with an experience that you originally suppressed because it was so painful, then rebirthing can be pure hell while you're waiting for that integration. When both the rebirther and the rebirthee have a thorough understanding of what makes integration happen, then material can be integrated when it is still at a very subtle level of manifestation, almost immediately after it comes into conscious awareness. This adds greatly to the client's sense of comfort and safety with the rebirthing process.

I use the term *integration* instead of the term *release* because release implies the letting go of something bad. The truth is that there is never anything bad to let go of; thinking that something bad needed to be gotten rid of is what caused suppression to happen in the first place. Rebirthing can be called "the science of loving all of yourself." This includes all the things you once decided to think of as wrong or bad.

Suppression and Integration

Integration is the opposite of suppression.

You can always make anything good or bad, pleasant or unpleasant. It has nothing at all to do with the thing itself and everything to do with your decision about it. If you insist on believing that anything is bad, then this is the same as insisting on having an unpleasant pattern of energy in your body. For instance, if you insist for any reason that you don't like punk rock music, then the bargain you're signing yourself up for includes having an unpleasant feeling in your physical body every time you hear it or even think about it. The music is the same whether you like it or not. If, sometime when you're hearing punk rock music, you decide to enjoy the feeling you get from it, then this is exactly the same as changing your decision about how good or bad it is. It works the same way for everything—

including communists, stomachaches, and family fights. A decision to love is always a decision to feel good and it's always 100% up to you.

Suppression is the process of deciding that something is unpleasant and then withdrawing awareness from it in an effort to feel good.

Integration is the process of allowing yourself to become aware of something you once suppressed and choosing to enjoy it.

Every thought has a corresponding pattern of energy in the body and a corresponding pattern of manifestation in one's life. For example, if a man has the thought "driving is dangerous," this thought will cause fear in his body and traffic accidents in his life. If he suppresses the fear he experiences, the thought will become unquestioned reality, the fear will become unconscious tension, and the traffic accidents he will experience (both his own and other people's) will reinforce his negative belief. This vicious circle is what makes some people accident-prone. The man in the example could change this pattern any time he chose, either by using the affirmation "driving is safe," or by getting rebirthed and integrating fear.

The suppression of any experience always involves the suppression of a corresponding negative belief. A negative belief is any thought which has both of two components: "It's unfortunate that it's that way (unpleasantness), but that's just the way it's got to be (choicelessness)." When a belief is suppressed it is no longer experienced as a belief; it is experienced as reality. The more someone tries to tell you about "the hard realities of life," or some such thing, the more suppressed material that person has. It's a lot like putting on a pair of sunglasses and then forgetting you have them on—you adjust yourself to a dark world and that's that.

Another way of describing suppression is in terms of the relationship between your physical body and your spirit body. Your spirit body is the body you have in your dreams. It includes your mind and all your conscious awareness. During dreaming you do not experience your physical body because your spirit body is not *in* your physical body. When you are awake, you experience your physical body to the extent that your spirit body is in contact with it. Some people have much more body awareness than others.

Suppression, in these terms, is the longterm withdrawal of the spirit body from areas of the physical body where something is happening which one has chosen not to experience.

If you decide to withdraw your awareness from an unpleasant experience you've created for yourself, what you are actually doing is withdrawing your spirit body from part of your physical body. The unpleasant pattern of energy will still keep happening in your physical body just as much as ever, but you will no longer be aware of it, except indirectly.

The spirit body is what organizes a bunch of molecules into the neat form we call "your physical body." The withdrawal of the spirit body from areas of the physical body, because of suppression, results in a blockage of vital organizing energy to that part of the physical body. The molecules become less well-organized, a condition we call "aging" or "sickness." The areas of blocked energy inevitably affect other parts of the body. If the person decides that these areas feel unpleasant too, this creates more suppression and more blocked energy, and so on.

Similarly, every negative belief has a built-in limitation that will decrease one's effectiveness at getting what one wants. For example, if I have the negative belief that chocolate milk isn't good for me, then either I won't drink it even if I want it, or else I will and I'll get a bad result from it. Limitation results in getting what one doesn't want, which experience can be made unpleasant and then suppressed, leading to more limitation.

In this way, suppression, once begun, usually results in the buildup of layer upon layer of suppression and the more-or-less steady withdrawal of the spirit body from the physical body. Death is caused by suppressing all the way out. Almost everybody begins suppressing at birth. If you don't remember your birth, then you know that you began suppressing at that time. Later I shall explain in detail how you can use integration to break this fatal chain of events.

Exactly how do people suppress things? There are several ways. Drugs are a popular way. Recreational drugs, prescription drugs, and the anesthesia given by hospitals and dentists are all excellent ways to cause suppression. Although not everybody gets the same result, generally alcohol suppresses fear, nicotine suppresses anger, marijuana suppresses sadness, and caffeine suppresses the long-lasting, energy-sapping results of anesthesia and other forms of suppression. If you use any of these substances habitually, try stopping abruptly for two weeks if you want to find out whether you have been using the substance to suppress. If you're honest with yourself, just *thinking* about stopping for two weeks may be enough to tell you the answer.

To get an idea of how this works, consider that anger causes dilation of the blood vessels, making a person turn red in the face. Nicotine causes the blood vessels to contract, thus suppressing a normal physiological feeling of anger. An observant person can see the suppressed anger in the body language of cigarette smokers, particularly in younger ones who have not yet learned to suppress body language. If you wish to quit smoking, I recommend using affirmations like: "My anger is a lovable part of me"; "It is OK for me to experience my anger now"; and especially, forgiveness affirmations in the format "I, _____, forgive _____ for _____."

Similarly, fear causes contraction of the blood vessels, making a person go pale; alcohol dilates them. Go to a bar frequented by alcoholics and look at all the men there who would rather die than express fear. That's why drinking is macho— *machismo* is mainly about suppressing fear.

Regarding the suppression of anesthesia by caffeine addiction, this is very common. It doesn't seem to matter whether the person got general anesthesia at birth (when it was given to the mother) or later in life (in preparation for an operation), people who have had general anesthesia are very commonly addicted to caffeine and very commonly have the classical anesthesia pattern come up during their rebirthing sessions. I have also seen heavy use of alcohol, barbiturates, sedatives, antidepressants, opiates, and even marijuana connected to caffeine addiction and the anesthesia pattern. In addition, people who are very suppressed may feel a need for constant doses of caffeine just to function, because maintenance of their structure of suppression is taking so much of their energy. Suppression means diverting some of your energy to hold back other parts of your energy. It's very energy-consuming. People also use other stimulants such as cocaine, amphetamines, and sometimes nicotine in the same way that people use caffeine. Some people are addicted to daily hard exercise to achieve the same end.

LSD and other psychedelics work basically as "super-stimulants" in this context. The only reason why LSD allows people to experience otherwise unconscious parts of themselves is that it "suppresses the suppression." A way to verify this to consider the physical and mental condition of most people who have taken "large" doses of LSD frequently over long periods of time. Anything that promotes deterioration of the mind or body is suppressive.

Generally one can suppress almost anything with a stimulant, and stimulants are the most suppressive and widely used of all suppressive drugs.

I'm not writing a pharmacopeia, but this gives you an idea of how chemical suppression works. Generally, if it makes you feel "different," it is suppressive. Integration means feeling "the same" and enjoying it.

Other popular suppressive techniques include habitual distraction (watching TV, sleeping, overeating) and telling lies, either to oneself or to others. Add your own favorites to the list.

Suppression is always accompanied by either the holding of the breath or the control of the exhale. Observe how most people breathe when they are watching TV. It is virtually impossible to suppress while keeping the breathing connected and the exhale relaxed.

Rebirthing is the science of bringing the spirit body into full contact with the physical body. Rebirthing causes youthing of the physical body in every case.

The Five Elements of Rebirthing

The quality that must be present with rebirthing breathing to make an integration happen is called "surrender." This means dropping your defenses, ceasing the struggle that is necessary to keep suppressed material out of your awareness, and extending acceptance to all parts of your being. The purpose of the breathing is two-fold: it simultaneously brings the suppressed material into your awareness and "cellularizes" surrender.

Rebirthing is a single process which can best be described in terms of five components:

1. Circular breathing
2. Total relaxation
3. Awareness in detail
4. Integration into ecstasy
5. Do whatever you do because everything works

Whenever integration occurs, all five of these elements are present. Whenever all five of these elements are present, integration occurs. I shall explain each one in detail.

Circular Breathing, the First Element of Rebirthing

"Circular breathing" means any kind of breathing that meets these three criteria:
1. The inhale and the exhale are connected together with no pauses anywhere.
2. The exhale is relaxed and not controlled at all.
3. Either the inhale and exhale are both through the nose or the inhale and exhale are both through the mouth. In through one and out through the other is not circular breathing.

The breath is the link between the spirit body and the physical body.

Circular breathing causes "complete circuits of energy" in the body, which you can feel, so it has the effect of bringing all parts of the body to a person's awareness. This is tantamount to bringing the spirit body into contact with the physical body. Suppressed material becomes "activated," which means it begins to affect the rebirthee's conscious awareness instead of just affecting the person from an unconscious level.

If you didn't know anything about rebirthing besides how to do circular breathing, and if you kept at it long enough, eventually you would achieve integration. Probably you would have a very uncomfortable experience. The breathing would activate material that you originally suppressed because it was unpleasant. Without using the other four elements, the material would be just as unpleasant this time around. If you kept doing circular breathing, the material would not go back into suppression but would keep becoming more and more activated. Eventually you would either stop doing circular breathing, in which case the material would gradually go back into suppression, or else you would decide that it was never going to go away anyhow, in which case you would surrender and integrate it. The other four elements enable you to surrender right from the start, which turns rebirthing into an extremely pleasant experience of going into deeper and deeper states of ecstasy as layer after layer of suppressed discomfort integrates.

Any type of breathing that is circular by the definition I have given will produce the rebirthing breathing effect. Different types of circular breathing do affect the body's energy in different ways, however, and certain types are especially appropriate in certain situations. The variables involved are: how much air is taken, how fast it is taken, whether it is taken through the nose or the mouth, and which part of the lungs it is taken into.

Full-lung breathing has the effect of sending maximum energy through the body and thus it brings suppressed material especially well to the person's awareness. It is especially helpful when the rebirthee is "going off into thoughts" or is otherwise having a difficult time staying "in the body." Sometimes, however, a pattern of energy comes up very strongly so that the person has no problem at all experiencing it. At these times very full breathing would not generally be recommended because it would bring the pattern up so strongly that it would make it hard for the rebirthee to relax.

Rapid circular breathing speeds up the exchange of energy through the complete circuits of energy in the body and thus can speed up the cellularization of the integration once the pattern has come thoroughly to the person's awareness. Rapid, shallow, circular breathing is often very helpful when a pattern is coming up very strongly and the integration is being delayed by not relaxing or by refusing to acknowledge ecstasy.

I suspect that 99 percent of people who have been rebirthed have had some "tetany," the temporary tightening of muscles in some part of the body. There is nothing at all dangerous or wrong about a rebirthee going into   perventilation and tetany. However, it is worth stating that hyperventilation is not necessary to the rebirthing process. The cause of hyperventilation is forcing or "blowing" the exhale. Relaxing the exhale is what allows the energy from the inhale to return from all parts of the body and make the complete circuit. If more energy is going into the body than is coming out, the result is a build-up of energy that causes the muscles of the affected area to contract. Because of tension stored in the chest from birth trauma, many people cannot completely relax their exhales, no matter how clear they are that it's the right way to breathe. These people get some tetany in their first few rebirthings. When they integrate their chest tension, the tetany goes away forever. There are times when good breathing instructions from the rebirther can minimize the tetany or bypass it altogether and thus allow quicker integration.

When suppressed anesthesia is coming up strongly, which feels like being heavily drugged, then the best breathing is both rapid and full, the fastest breathing possible, since anesthesia is a very strong pattern of energy and makes it difficult to stay in the body. If the goal is to produce the maximum result in the minimum time, then the rebirthee with anesthesia coming up should keep breathing as fast and full as possible, no matter what, even if it means standing up or bathing in cold water to stay conscious.

Anesthesia is not the only thing that can make a person tend to go unconscious during rebirthing. With some things it might occasionally be helpful just to let the person sleep briefly, and with anesthesia it is sometimes tempting to do so, but my reserach definitely shows that quicker results are achieved by keeping the person awake and breathing.

Whenever a person suppresses anything, the body must put a new inhibition into the breathing mechanism in order to keep the energy suppressed, sort of like putting a dam in a river. Different instances of suppression put blocks in different areas of the lungs, chest, shoulders, and abdominal muscles, and the trachea, sinuses, nose and mouth. Most of the suppression that occurs at birth inhibits the breathing in the upper lungs. For this reason, upper lung breathing usually activates the most material for people who are relatively new to rebirthing. From simple observation, one can discern where a person's breathing is inhibited. Guiding a person to breathe there usually causes the activation of a corresponding pattern of energy in the person's body.

Regarding nose versus mouth breathing during rebirthing, the basic rule is "whatever feels better is better." The mouth is a bigger orifice and when more air is desirable or when the nose is blocked with congestion, then mouth breathing is preferred. In general, however, most people relax more deeply when they breathe through their noses.

Whenever a person integrates anything, the breathing releases somewhat. The classical breathing release happens when a person integrates memory of the first breath, but everyone experiences as many breathing releases as they do integrations.

Total Relaxation, the Second Element of Rebirthing

It takes a lot of effort to keep something suppressed! Many times, small movements, muscle tightenings, the changing of positions, fidgeting, etc., are the distractions necessary to keep suppressed material from coming to a person's awareness. When the whole body is relaxed, the areas that will not relax come much more readily to conscious awareness.

In general, I recommend that the rebirthee get into one comfortable position and stay there, without moving, fidgeting, or scratching itches, throughout the whole session. I have very many times seen unscratched itches become surprising and important patterns of energy. In dry rebirthing, lying on the back, legs uncrossed, palms up at the sides, in a position of complete vulnerability, is usually best. Instead of moving or scratching, one thus gets a chance to really feel what it is like to *want* to do these things. This is one of the best ways I know to activate material quickly and integrate it subtly.

Sometimes a person will get very relaxed during a rebirthing session; then suddenly he will start to feel like he's so relaxed that if he gets any more relaxed he's going to jump right out of his skin! When this happens, it means that a new pattern of energy is starting to be activated. Of course the person should just keep relaxing.

The "drama," such as crying, screaming, vomiting, or crawling around, which sometimes accompanies the activation of a pattern of energy, is OK and certainly not to be avoided if it comes up spontaneously, but it does not cause integration. Indeed, very often it distracts a rebirthee from really feeling what's happening and thus makes the integration take longer and be more difficult than it needed to be.

It should be pointed out here that expressing an emotion is not the opposite of suppressing it. If a person has anger, he will do better to take responsibility for it and apply the five elements to it than he will to go around expressing his old hostility to everybody he meets. The expression of an emotion can be the distraction necessary to keep it suppressed. This is true especially often with anger, but also sometimes with sadness and fear.

Laughter, generally speaking, is not drama. More about this later on.

One of the most important reasons to use the five elements is that they enable a person to integrate material at a much subtler level than would otherwise be possible. Total relaxation is very important to this because commonly the first awareness that a person has of some suppressed energy is awareness of an area of the body that will not relax.

Relaxation is very important in the actual moment of integration as well, because at that moment, energy that has been made wrong and held away from the body's normal energy is re-accepted and the very cells of the body drop their struggle against it. A good way to describe rebirthing is "a relaxation technique so effective that the tension never comes back."

Obviously rebirthing does not have to be done on one's back. When people are integrating massive fear or massive sadness, it is often best for them to curl up in a fetal ball. When anesthesia is coming up, sitting and sometimes even standing is helpful. Various positions are good in tub rebirthing. In very advanced sessions, I even guide clients into integration while they are driving a car or eating in a restaurant. In all cases, however, total relaxation is of key importance in bringing about integration.

Awareness in Detail, the Third Element of Rebirthing

During rebirthing, one wants to bring one's awareness as much as possible into the present moment to explore everything in the here and now in the greatest possible detail.

A "pattern of energy" can be anything. It can be tingling in your toes, a choir of cats yowling in the alleyway, or remembering the smell of your grandmother's cookies. My quick definition is: any discrete experience that is part of a person's subjective reality in a given moment in time.

In the course of rebirthing, the patterns of energy change. Suppression is in layers, rather like layers of an onion, with each layer covering up the layers beneath it. Integrating one layer usually activates the next layer down.

Patterns of energy also change because sometimes component parts of a larger pattern get activated separately. For instance, if you were integrating a suppressed experience of being dropped by a nurse when you were an infant, first might come fear, then the thought that you can't trust women, and then pain, and then it might all come together as an integrative memory. Often when components are coming up separately, awareness will switch around among them for a while.

It's a good idea to keep awareness of the whole body while rebirthing. As a natural process, some things will come to a person's awareness more than others. Whatever comes is exactly what the rebirthee should most put his awareness into, experience in detail at that moment.

It is also best to be aware of "external" things, rather than try to screen them out. Obviously people get activated by things in their environment and just as obviously they are the source of everything in their experience; so the jet noises, or the rowdy children, or the sound of other people rebirthing nearby, are important parts of a rebirthing session.

Anytime something starts to "distract" a rebirthee, the "distraction" is actually the pattern of energy that's coming up for the person right then — the one to focus on and experience in detail.

Integration into Ecstasy, the Fourth Element of Rebirthing

I shall explain this element in several ways because I have found that people differ in the ways they most easily understand it.

The Ecstasy Principle is this: *Everybody is always in a state of ecstasy whether they like it or not.*

By *ecstasy* I do not mean an emotion. The word *ecstasy* comes from the ancient Greek *ek stasis*, one translation of which is "standing apart." You know you're not your mind or your body, because you are *experiencing* your mind and your body. You are pure Experiencer, standing apart from any of the things you are experiencing. At this level, there is no judgement of good or bad, right or wrong, pleasant or unpleasant. There is also no time. There *is* the experience of your *mind* creating these things.

You, the Soul, the Experiencer, are always in a state of ecstasy, regardless of anything your mind or body may be going through. Awareness is ecstasy.

A corollary of the Ecstasy Principle is this: Either you're enjoying what you're experiencing, or you're enjoying not enjoying it, or you're enjoying not enjoying not enjoying it—I've never had to go backward beyond this point to get agreement from anybody about anything in their experience.

This means that anything that comes up in a rebirthing session, regardless of what judgement was placed on it at the time it was originally suppressed, is already being enjoyed ecstatically by you at one level or another.

The fourth element says: *Experience everything from a place where you are already enjoying it.*

Here are some other ways of explaining it. There exist an infinite number of ways to enjoy anything. Find ones that work for everything in your experience.

1. Give everything in your experience total, loving acceptance.
2. Keep your sense of humor about everything you're experiencing.
3. Love yourself for experiencing everything that's coming up for you.
4. Since you know that your thoughts are the only source of everything in your personal reality, then everything you experience is the satisfaction of a desire of yours. The part of you that desired the result you are getting now is in a state of fulfillment. Experience that.
5. Totally celebrate everything in your experience.
6. Be very enthusiastic about everything. If you're afraid, really get into being afraid; if you're sad, get enthusiastically sad; etc.

The only thing that exists is pleasure. If you have an experience and decide that it's unpleasant, you have told a lie. Suppression is the system of lies necessary to maintain that original lie. As soon as you rebirth and acknowledge that the experience is really pleasurable, the truth has been told! The whole system of lies disappears! In other words, the only suppression in your body is suppressed pleasure.

The way to get the fourth element that seems to work best for most people is gratitude. Everyone has an experience of being grateful for existing, for being here to experience anything. Most people have a boundary to their experience of gratitude, however, and they will acknowledge being grateful for some things but not others. The fourth element says: *The present moment is all you've got — be grateful for every detail of it!*

Here is a game that will help you understand the fourth element. It's called:

Creating Your Own Reality

Rules: 1. Create things that already exist.
2. Put things where they already are.
3. Be flamboyant, mystical, and pompous about doing it.

Thus:

"I *command* the Universe to put a book about rebirthing into my hands, NOW!"

"Let there be *light* to shine on this book!".

"I command the earth to bring forth *trees!* And let them be grouped together in *forests* and also scattered about singly and in small groups in people's *yards!*"

Play this game when you're getting rebirthed, thus:

"Let there be tingling in my hands!"

"I command that there shall be a craving for *hamburgers* in my *mouth* and *throat* and *stomach!*"

"Let there be *doubt!*"
And so on.

In other words, pretend that you are intentionally creating your experience just the way it is because you like it that way. Acknowledge yourself; you have created a perfect universe.

Do Whatever You Do, Because Everything Works, the Fifth Element of Rebirthing

At first I tried to use just four elements of rebirthing but it didn't work. People lay there trying to integrate things instead of actually integrating them. The purpose of the fifth element is to integrate trying to integrate. It is meant to be taken literally. If you're always in a state of ecstasy how can you do anything wrong?

How to Know When You've Integrated Something

One metaphysical way to explain rebirthing is that it causes the integration of dualities. For example, if you think sadness is the opposite of happiness, then you have a duality. This means that somewhere inside you, you have a little scale that looks like this:

10   Very Happy
9
8
7
6
5
4
3
2
1
0   Very Sad

If you are like this, then you will suppress sadness, one way or another, whenever it comes up. You'll think a thought that makes you sad and then you'll begin a mad scramble to get back to the happy end of the scale. Perhaps you'll use a drug, distractions, or self-delusion. It doesn't matter—the results will be the same: (1) The sad thought will become accepted as reality instead of just a thought; (2) you'll add to the slush fund of suppressed sadness that you carry around in your body; and, (3) you will again and again create sad situations for yourself, because (4) your sad thoughts will continue to create your reality, and (5) your build-up of suppressed sadness will seek an outlet.

If you are like this, then when you get rebirthed you will start getting in touch with your sadness. At first you may try to suppress your sadness, but as you continue breathing, your sadness will come up more and more. As you keep relaxing and going into it, you will experience sadness for what it is—a particular sensation of energy in your body. As you apply the fourth element, you will begin to enjoy feeling the sadness and by the end of the session, you will be feeling better and more energetic than you have in years, perhaps ever. After rebirthing, whenever sadness comes up you will enjoy your feeling of sadness and experience it fully instead of suppressing it. Then you can be happy even when you're sad, thus integrating this duality, so that your sad part and your happy part can work together, but independently, like this:

```
0  1  2  3  4  5  6  7  8  9  10
Not very happy                Very happy

0  1  2  3  4  5  6  7  8  9  10
Not very sad                  Very sad
```

You know that you have integrated something when you no longer resist it. Either it won't happen any more, or else it will and you'll enjoy it.

How to Apply the Five Elements to Anything

Rebirthing is applying the five elements to your body, integrating your body's suppression. You can also apply the five elements to: your love life, your finances, losing weight and everything else.

For instance, if you have a habit of bouncing checks, then you can apply the five elements like this.

1.   Relax and connect up your breathing.
2.   Now, examine everything about your experience of bouncing checks. Some possible methods of doing this could be: Get out all the little red overdraft notices you've gotten from your bank and all the angry letters you've gotten from the people to whom you wrote bad checks. Make visual aids, like charts showing the times of the month with the most bounced checks or graphs of how many people in each category got them from you. Do you bounce the most checks to creditors? to grocery stores? to bartenders? Make lists: "All the reasons why I sometimes bounce checks," "Benefits I get from sometimes writing bad checks," "Disadvantages of bouncing checks," etc. Total up how much it's cost you. Draw cartoons of yourself giving people bad checks, then burn them up and draw new cartoons of yourself putting money in the bank, or paying for everything with cash, or carefully tallying up your check stubs after writing each check. Make up your own processes. Notice all your feelings.

Keep your sense of humor and a sense of honest detachment while doing this. If you're making yourself wrong then love yourself for making yourself wrong. If it makes you feel afraid, then be afraid! If it makes you feel dumb, then go ahead! BE DUMB!

Then do whatever you do, and that will work.

Integration Affirmations

In general, affirmations are the opposite side of the same coin from rebirthing: Rebirthing is about surrendering to what's so, and affirmations are about telling what's so how to be. There are, however, affirmations that aid in integration:

1. All statements are equally true.
2. Everything is better than everything else.
3. Everybody is better than everybody else.
4. It is OK for _____ to _____.
5. _____ exists for my convenience and pleasure.
6. Everything is perfect and so is everything else.
7. All sensations in my body are pleasurable.
8. I am safe.
9. I am good.
10. Everything is good.
11. I have infinite ability to enjoy anything.
12. My whole body is a pleasure organ.
13. I love everything about myself.
14. I love everything about _____.
15. The purpose of life is to have fun.
16. _____ is always one of my favorite pleasures.
17. Every part of me is enthusiastically doing what's best for every part of me.
18. I am grateful for _____.
19. _____ is _____ enough.
20. Everything is evolving as it should.

Laughter, by the way, is an expression of the pattern of energy that happens in your body when you integrate a paradox.

The purpose of rebirthing is to have fun.

An Introduction to Rebirthing for Health Professionals*

Eve Jones, Ph.D.

I'm greatly pleased to be introducing you to a simple technique you can use both to reduce your own stress reactions as you care for your patients and that you can teach to your patients to facilitate their healing.

This technique, called Conscious Connected Breathing, or Rebirthing, has been in use in the USA since the mid-70s, and it has proved itself effective in a remarkably wide variety of disorders, including not only mental or emotional problems, but also acute and chronic physical ailments. It has also led to some profound spiritual experiences in many of the thousands who have already practiced this technique.

Now, you're probably turned off by claims that any specific technique is curative in a variety of disorders that ostensibly have nothing in common. This sounds too much like the claims of the people last century who sold snake oil for every sort of ailment, both in people and in livestock. If you're accustomed to thinking of disease as being caused primarily by a single pathogen, it's reasonable for you to reject "snake oil" claims. but if you take the approach that every cause of disease ultimately effects its pathogenic changes on a few dominent physiological processes, then the broad effectiveness of Rebirthing becomes more understandable, for it appears to exert its greatest effect on two simple processes: (1) the rate at which the body builds and maintains healthy tissue which performs its functions normally, and (2) the rate at which metabolic wastes are eliminated from the cells and fluids of the body.

Vitality or good health is related to the rate at which the body turns over energy in these anabolic and catabolic functions. The faster we make or repair or replace old body stuff, the healthier we are. And the faster we eliminate wastes produced by such work or by tissue breakdown, the more easily the body keeps itself in good order. The body's homeostatic mechanisms work marvelously well, especially if we aren't gunking ourselves up with substances the body was never designed to handle, toxins like refined carbohydrates, caffeine, and nicotine or the heavy metals that pollute our air and water. When we aren't getting rid of wastes and toxins at the same rate that we're taking them in or making them in ourselves, we gradually accumulate deposits of such substances, often in fat cells. And eventually, our body mechanisms become sufficiently upset so that disease ensues. One of those diseases may even be the condition known as old age. Thus, hypothetically, disease can be resisted and old age can be delayed or partially reversed by providing to the body a sufficiency of the building blocks it uses, free of pollutants, and by maximizing the effectiveness with which the body eliminates accumulated wastes and keeps up to current production.

In this connection, it's important to recognize the part played by simple respiration, not as the means by which we take in the oxygen which enables us to perform all the body work, but as a means of eliminating wastes from the body.

Surprisingly, only 3% of total body wastes are eliminated via defecation and only 7% via urination. The skin passes out another 20%, leaving the remaining 70% to be breathed out. I'm not disputing the importance of a high bulk diet and plenty of water or of working up a good sweat; I'm merely calling attention to the immense amount of work that breathing performs. It obviously behooves us to breathe fully and freely and to breathe clean air.

Yet, when we investigate breathing, we find that most people aren't breathing most of the time! They tend to take their inhale as a short gasp which they hold for a while before exhaling in a long exhale and then they stay collapsed on the exhale for another long pause before starting the next gasp in. The amount of time they spend both inhaling and exhaling is shorter than the time they spend not doing either.

Modern medicine advocates bringing up the respiration rate and breathing into all available lung space by performing aerobic exercise which also increases heart rate. Such cardiopulmonary exercise for 30 minutes a day correlates well with keeping the arteries clear of plaque that may contribute to hypertension or to embolisms. Since half of the deaths each day in the USA are associated with hypertension, and since hypertension is less likely to develop in a person who exercises vigorously each day, bringing up the heart and respiratory rate appears to have positive results.

Unfortunately, vigorous exercise cannot be recommended for the old and infirm and diseased, for their bodies are already burdened, so they cannot handle the extra labor of disposing of the added wastes exercise produces. Indeed, if their building-up processes are slowed down, exercise may even break down irreplaceable muscle mass. So, the very people who most need the benefits regular vigorous exercise can produce cannot enjoy it and obtain the benefits.

Fortunately, our breath is under our control partially and our body reflexly alters heart rate as respiratory rate changes. So we can have the benefits of safely increasing heart rate, without producing new metabolites to labor our body with, simply by concentrating our consciousness on our breath and breathing more fully than previously.

And that is exactly what Rebirthing is all about: It is, primarily, a way of breathing which can be learned in a few sessions and which can then be practiced constantly. So, whenever you are stressed, you can Rebirth to release tension. Whenever you're tired, you can Rebirth to re-vitalize yourself. And you can teach this breathing to all your patients to help them recover and to promote their own health. It is easy to learn and easy to practice, and it is also safe.

So, to describe Rebirthing briefly, it's a breathing technique in which the Rebirthee inhales deeply and fully, with special attention to drawing the breath high into the chest, into the lung space that is usually not used, and then, immediately and without any pause to hold on to the inhale, lets it go, without any forcing or pushing or shaping of the stream of air. The breathing is continuous, without any pauses or holding of air, either of the inhale or the exhale. The exhale is effortless and brief, being only the release of breath as tension is no longer maintained in the intercostal muscles lifting the rib cage or in the diaphragm which has been pulling down. As these muscles collapse, the chest snaps out the exhale.

Such a pattern of breathing is *not* hyperventilation. It is simply a pattern that allows the individual to breath all the time, not just for part of the time. it opens up previously unused lung space, so it can be called "superventilation," but because the exhale is not forced or prolonged, there is none of the excessive blowing off of CO_2 that is the cause of the hyperventilation syndrome. Hyperventilation occurs when the partial pressure of CO_2 in the blood circulating to the brain stem is so low that it is below the threshold for stimulation of the inspiration center located in the brain stem. The center thus doesn't trigger off another inspiration until the partial pressure of CO_2 accumulates and passes the threshold value. As the person who has been blowing out forcibly feels breathless during the long pause before the pCO_2 builds up, he experiences a psychological state we call panic. And in his panic, he pushes himself to take another breath and then pushes even more on the next exhale, thus compounding the problem. The acid-base balance in the blood stream adjusts to the lowering of the pCO_2 and a condition known as alkalosis develops, characterized by tetany and muscular spasm, often to the point of producing intense pain in the strained muscles and joints.

One treatment of hyperventilation is to have the person breathe into a container, for example, his cupped hands or a paper bag, so that he breathes air that has a high partial pressure of CO_2 — his respiratory centers are properly stimulated, he stops being breathless, and his panic passes, but only temporarily, for he's likely to start forcing the exhale again and re-create the same situation again.

Thousands of perfect Rebirths have been conducted without the Rebirthees getting involved in hyperventilation. But it is true that people who are afraid of the feelings and thoughts within them start to push on the exhale, as if they were ridding the body of something bad. So the less relaxed a Rebirthee is about the entire process, the more likely he is to suffer the inconveniences of hyperventilation. Eventually, one of two things will happen: (1) he continues to breathe, following the direction of his Rebirther, and the entire attack of hyperventilation melts away, or (2) he holds his breath and finishes the session after resuming his breathing and conforming to the requirement of keeping the breath continuous and circular. In either case, the attack of hyperventilation has caused no lasting harm. Moreover, as the Rebirthee moves through the spastic phase, he learns that he can let go, and he stops hyperventilating in the face of stress. Deep breathing when aroused, yes, but forced exhaling, no.

In short, the superventilation of Rebirthing appears to cure the hyperventilation attack, and make it no longer necessary for the person to produce an attack again.

So, any apprehensions you may have had because of confusing the Rebirth process with hyperventilation can be discarded. Rebirthing is safe and painless in the majority of cases and it does not necessarily involve hyperventilation.

Leonard Orr, the originator of Rebirthing, regards the breath as the natural healing mechanism because, as we maintain the continuous breathe for an hour or so, we slip out of the here-and-now state of consciousness and we recognize, flitting through our mind, old images and old feelings. And as we continue the connected breathing, these seem to leave consciousness and no longer have any psychological charge. We can hypothesize that this natural healing mechanism is effective to the extent that it's in use, that is, that, since most people don't breath consciously and in a connected manner most of the time, their breathing isn't used to heal most of the time. But the mechanism is there, ready to be revived and utilized whenever the person overcomes whatever unwillingness exists to using it.

For that seems to be the central issue — the reason we don't breathe in the connected pattern constantly, as contented animals appear to do and as people in deep sleep do, is that we cling to our attachment to emotional, charged reactions and we are afraid to give them up, as we would promptly do in the course of breathing consciously. And Leonard Orr states that the reason we cling to such old emotional reactions is that we connect them with survival, as a consequence of the circumstances of our birth. Most people, throughout history, have not been conceived, carried, or born as conscious acts of love — instead, lots of negatives are usually involved. Life, itself, was so "nasty, brute, and short" for most of mankind's history, that love was almost of necessity confounded with anxiety or worse. And when technological advances made enough differences in the Western world to provide more luxurious expectations of plenty, those same advances took away from mothers their opportunity to give birth in love. The men of medicine took over with their anesthetics and forceps and turned birthing into an event regarded as an ordeal, moreover, one in which the anesthetized mother couldn't even play a conscious role. Queen Victoria was the first woman to give birth under general anesthetic, quite late in the 19th century, so for most of the past century, Western mothers have mainly given birth while unconscious and thus unable to strain or push to help the infant move down the birth canal and out of the pelvis. The baby, itself, shares the mother's anesthetic and so is less effective in its own behalf as it shoulders its way down and out and is also often depressed enough so that breathing starts more slowly. And the birthing personnel who themselves have similar birth-related anxieties step in to "rescue" the infant, often using painful stimulation to "get" the infant to take its first breath.

It's no surprise to me that most of us haven't been eager to re-experience such events filled with negatives, that most of us cling to our basic imprints that link survival with pain and with held breath, with being helpless, with being unconscious, with struggle.

It's extremely difficult, if not impossible, to remember the oldest imprints we have stored in our consciousness simply by turning our attention to them. That's because there's so much charge on these imprints that coming close to them frightens the individual into holding the breath or hurts the individual into holding the breath. Whatever the emotion, if it isn't delicious joyful recollection, breathing becomes disrupted.

As you can easily see, therefore, it's necesary to have another person present usually during the early Rebirthing sessions, mainly to remind the Rebirthee to breathe when old imprints come to consciousness and interfere with the connected pattern. Once the Rebirthee has let go the old charged material, once the breathing has eliminated the old charged material along with the water and CO_2, the connected breathing isn't interrupted by old pains and sorrows and fears and rages and shames and guilts and anxieties. Thus, the connected breathing does its job of letting go the negatives, thereby promoting healing and growth.

The mechanism of action of the breath in opening up old imprints to consciousness in the here and now isn't understood. Possibly it's because the connected breathing provides for the brain the same milieu that prevailed during most of gestation when placental exchange ensured the fetus continual supply of oxygen and constant, prompt removal of wastes. Although the mother may have had all sorts of thoughts and emotions that produced chemicals which may well have crossed the placental barrier and that interfered with the mother's connected breathing rhythm, the osmotic exchange through the placenta was constant rather than intermittant as it is for most people prior to their Rebirthing session when they finally let go the imprinted connection between emotion and breathing. Until that imprint is dissolved, a Rebirthee does well to have a trained, competent, sensitive, successful Rebirther present during the session.

Perhaps the breathing "works" because connected, deep breathing opens up not only lung space that has been paralyzed with remembered fear but also capillary beds in the deep substance of the brain, in the limbic system, the tissue that surrounds the lateral ventricles. Or perhaps the connected breathing causes changes across the blood-brain barrier so that the cerebrospinal fluid in the lateral ventricles become identical to its composition chemically during gestation and birth. Modern science dictates that when circumstances are identical, identical events occur. So the cells of the limbic system which hold the imprints in the memory-RNA may let the memory trace break down when the fluid milieu becomes identical to what it was when the RNA was manufactured.

Whatever the specific mechanisms of action that operate in the Rebirthing may be, the evidence of its effectiveness is widespread. To date, the thousands of people who have become Rebirthers have been involved in helping thousands of people with significant physical problems including acne, alcoholism, angina, anorexia nervosa, arthritis, asthma, barbiturate addiction, bulimia, caffeine addiction, chronic bronchitis, diabetes, digestive disorders, epilepsy, hypertension, menstrual disorders, nicotine addiction, obesity, opiate addiction, poor peripheral circulation, post-traumatic paralysis, sexual disorders, spastic paralysis, tranquilizer addiction, and upper respiratory disorders. Patients with allergies, cancers, duodenal ulcers, gastric ulcers, kidney problems, and migraines have been Rebirthed successfully, and the assessment of their long-term condition is not yet completed. In addition to this wide variety of physical ailments, every type of neurotic and psychotic personality disorder have been Rebirthed successfully and have made major personality changes for the better within a matter of a few sessions.

Because the people who have become Rebirthers are drawn from every profession and vocation, record keeping has not been scientific, nor has there been a great deal of concern with establishing the initial diagnosis and condition. It is hoped that as you use this technique with your own patients, you will help to remedy the problems involved with establishing the evidence of its effectiveness.

With reference to the personality changes that even one Rebirthing session produces, it should be mentioned that it is common for Rebirthees to reawaken former religious feelings or even develop new religious and spiritual attitudes. This is especially likely in cases involving healings of so-called irreversible conditions. So, in addition to providing for the material benefit of your patients by teaching them the Rebirthing technique, you may even be instrumental in promoting another source of ease and peace.

If you are interested in a further discussion of the relation between the birth and the development of negative belief systems or if you are interested in learning how to Rebirth, please write to me and I will be pleased to recommend to you a Rebirth training you can attend. Similarly, if you don't know a Rebirther close to you, please write and I will send you a list of trained Rebirthers in your locality. I am also pleased to send you a list of publications that discuss the Rebirthing philosophy and related topics, including underwater birth.

I hope I have communicated to you my sincere recommendation of Rebirthing as a safe, easy, pleasant, rational, effective method of bringing healing to the body, the mind, the heart, and the soul. It profoundly alters the relationship between the healed and the healer. I am totally confident you will find it everything you ever dreamt of when you first considered taking care of others for your vocation. Thank you. In Peace, Simplicity, and Love, Breathe!

Dr. Eve Jones received her scientific training at the University of Chicago where she earned a Bachelor of Science degree in Chemistry, a Master of Science in Physiology and General Biology, and a Doctorate in Clinical Psychology. She has also done extensive post-graduate work in endocrinology and in neuropharmacology. She taught psychology at the University of Chicago for eight years and then moved to Los Angeles where she has been teaching college for the past 20 years, in addition to maintaining her private practice in psychoanalytically-oriented psychotherapy, including seven years of primal therapy and the past four years of Rebirthing. The mother of four grown children and of one granddaughter to date, she is well known as a writer on parent-child interactions. So she is

uniquely qualified to examine Rebirthing and to present a considered introduction to it to scientifically-oriented individuals.

(This material is available separately as a booklet at a cost of
$1.00 and as a 30-minute tape at a cost of $5.00. To order, please
send the appropriate amount, plus $1.75 per order, plus .35¢ per
item, and 6½ % sales tax in California, c/o Life Unlimited Book
Service, 8125 Sunset Avenue, Suite 204, Fair Oaks, CA 95628.)

Rebirther's Prayer

Breathe

Open up your lungs and heart
and let God's energy flow through you

Allow the Infinite power to heal
years of pain and sorrow
replacing them with
love
and joy
and peace

How insanely simple a process
and yet how arduous the path
that finally brought us here

Breathe
and let love fill your body and soul

Breathe
and allow fears and uncertainty
to flow out of every pore

Breathe
and let God be with you

Appendix II:
Suggested Readings and Tapes

The following books and tapes contain some of the most valuable ideas to be found anywhere. I encourage you to use these products to further your growth and success. Reading and listening is a wonderful and effective way to use the suggestion principle. Take charge of your life. Deliberately build the consciousness you want now by reading and listening to these and other positive products. Surround yourself with good ideas.

I suggest that you pick one or more of these books and tapes that appeal to you and use it to expand your success. Get into the habit of self-improvement. A positive and enlightened consciousness is your most valuable possession.

Suggested Reading

Books by Sondra Ray

The Celebration of Breath
Sondra Ray

$7.95, paper, 204 pages
Celestial Arts, Berkeley, CA
This is the latest book on Rebirthing, sharing new advancements in Rebirthing, Breath Awareness and Healing.

Loving Relationships
Sondra Ray

$6.95, paper, 160 pages
Celestial Arts, Berkeley, CA
Gain deep insights into your relationships with your lover, parents, children, boss, friends and your relationship with yourself. Find out why your relationships turn out the way the do, and improve the quality of all your relationships.
CONTENTS INCLUDE: Part One: THE SECRETS. God. Get Enlightened. Use Affirmations. Get Rebirthed. Handle Your Unconscious Death Urge. Love Yourself. Love Your Body. Clear Up The Ten Patterns. Handle Old Relationships. The Highest Spiritual Thought. Purpose of Relationship. Surrender. Part Two: MORE ABOUT RELATIONSHIPS. Werner Erhard. Loving Relationships Training. Personal Accounts from the L.R.T. Part Three: RELATIONSHIPS WITH IMMORTALISTS. Bobby. Fred. Jim. Bob. Bill. The Making of A Trainer.
Those of you who have taken the Loving Relationships Training will immediately recognize these chapter headings.

Much of the book is directly from the information in the training, which Sondra has been developing and perfecting for years.

As with *I Deserve Love*, the book is very clearly and simply written, and designed for immediate and successful personal use.

I Deserve Love
Sondra Ray

$6.95, paper, 128 pages
Celestial Arts, Berkeley, CA
Love, sex, and relationships. Using affirmations to have what you want, and to expand your self-esteem. Affirmations are "positive thoughts you hold in mind to produce desired results." Why and how affirmations work is the powerful topic of this book. Through writing and stating affirmations, thought patterns become progressively more positive. You then tune in to the "universal consciousness," attracting those on higher and higher vibration levels. Affirmations such as "I deserve love," and "I deserve sexual pleasure," are shown to work in a matter of days. This is strikingly illustrated by the various case studies which Sondra presents throughout the book. The book is filled with positive ideas on sex, love, relationships and self-esteem.

The Only Diet There Is
Sondra Ray

$6.95, paper, 156 pages
Celestial Arts, Berkeley, CA
"Driving up the California coast one glorious winter day, Sondra Ray read me the text of this book. It was stunning. The message was so simple, so true, I was amazed it hadn't been written before. As often with Sondra's ideas, I volunteered to be the first 'subject,' the first tried-and-tested 'experiment.'

Would this really work? The next day I began this unusual diet. Life has never been quite the same. By the end of the week, I'd lost several pounds but, more important, I was so in love with life and myself I had the self-worth to create a beautiful body. Within one month I had lost fifteen pounds, achieving my perfect body weight. The theory is simple. Though we might think it is our negative eating habits that have kept us unattractive and unhealthy, it is really our negative thoughts and feelings."

From the Preface by Linda Thistle, Ph.D.

This book is about much more than weight and dieting. It is about improving your relationship with your self and your body.

The Truth About Psychology

From Here to Greater Happiness
Joel and Champion Teutsch

$2.95, paper, 176 pages
Price/Stern/Sloan, Los Angeles, CA
A clear and simple explanation of how the mind works. Examples of personal laws in action.

The Creative Process in the Individual
Thomas Troward

$7.95, cloth
Dodd, Mead & Co., N.Y., NY
This is an excellent book on metaphysics — how life works. Other books by the same author are good, too. (Dore' Lectures; Edinburgh Lectures; Bible Mystery & Bible Meaning)

Your Inner Child of the Past
Hugh Missildine

$2.95, paper
Simon and Schuster, N.Y., NY
This is a clear, loving psychological book about childhood. It gives case histories which you can use to locate you own childhood patterns.

Spiritual Psychology
Jim Morningstar, Ph.D.

$8.00, paper, 180 pages
Spiritual Psychology Press, Milwaukee, WI
A brilliant synthesis of Contemporary Psychology, Holistic Health, and Modern Metaphysics. An integration of the body, mind, and spirit for the new age.

Rebirthing

Rebirthing in the New Age
Leonard Orr and Sondra Ray

$9.95, paper, 320 pages
Celestial Arts, Berkeley, CA
This is the original book on Rebirthing. It is considered a necessary textbook for those interested in Rebirthing.

Rebirthing: The Science of Enjoying All Your Life
Phil Laut

$7.95, paper
Trinity Publications, San Rafael, CA
This book describes how rebirthing works in a simple and

detailed way. Contents include: The truth about being human; Rebirthing; How to create your reality; Your past and you; Immortalist philosophy; Your future and you.

Birth Without Violence
Dr. Frederic Leboyer

$11.95, cloth, 128 pages
Random House, Westminister, MD
Birth from the baby's viewpoint. Reading this book can help you remember your own birth and the first (nonverbal) conclusions you made about life. Beautifully written and illustrated with photographs of blissful and aware babies. This book is requried reading for the Rebirthing process. It is also an excellent book for anyone who is planning on being involved in the birth of a child. Rediscover the divine child within you.

Secret Life of the Unborn Child
Dr. Thomas Verny, M.D.

$6.95, paper
Summit Books, N.Y., NY
Synthesizing for the first time the latest findings from all scientific disciplines dealing with the unborn, including Dr. Verny's pioneering work in prenatal psychology. *The Secret Life of the Unborn Child* demonstrates that from the sixth month of intra-uterine life (and sometimes even earlier) the unborn child is a feeling, experiencing, remembering being who responds to and is deeply influenced by his environment.

Money and Prosperity

Money Is My Friend
Phil Laut

$5.00, paper
Trinity publications, San Rafael, CA
"One of the best books available about prosperity consciousness." The author probes every area of life that could be
blocking the reader from reaching his full potential. This book
covers the topic of "money in abundance" in depth.

Moneylove
Jerry Gillies

$2.95, paper
Warner Books, New York, NY
Particularly good for freeing up your attitudes about money.

The Richest Man in Babylon
George Clason

$2.95, paper, 160 pages
Bantam Books, New York, NY
A wonderful primer on the 4 laws of wealth. Recommended at
money seminars as the best basic book about money. Written in
parables. "A lean purse is easier to cure than to endure."

Physical Immortality
Leonard Orr

$9.95, paper, 80 pages
Celestial Arts, Berkeley, CA
In depth discussion of immortalist philosophy. An account of
the immortal master Herakahn Baba in India. Socological implications of physical immortality.

The Door of Everything
by Ruby Nelson

$3.95, paper, 180 pages
DeVorss & Co., Marina del Rey, CA
A wonderful statement of Immortalist Philosophy.

The Immortalist
Alan Harrington

$5.95, paper, 316 pages
Celestial Arts, Berkeley, CA
An alternative to the belief systems that accept and educate people for inevitable death. It proposes that "the time has come for man to get rid of the intimidating gods in his own head, to grow up out of his cosmic inferiority complex, to bring his disguised desire for eternal life into the open and go after what he really wants — the only state he will settle for — divinity." "Mr. Harrington may have written the most important book of our time." —Gore Vidal

Beyond Mortal Boundaries
Annalee Skarin

$4.95, paper, 356 pages
DeVorss & Co., Marina Del Rey, CA
Analee Skarin recognized the message of life eternal — physical immortality — through study of the Bible. Her book is an extremely power affirmation of life and the unlimited power of God through and in any person.

The Life and Teachings Of The Masters Of The Far East
Baird Spalding

$4.00 per volume, 5 volumes, paper
DeVorss & Co., Marina Del Rey, CA
An account of American scientists who visited and lived with

immortal masters in the Himalayas around the turn of the century. From the introduction:

"During our stay — 3½ years — we contacted the great masters of the Himilayas... They permitted us to enter into their lives intimately, and we were thus able to see the actual workings of the Great law as demonstrated by them... They supply everything needed for their daily wants directly from the universe, including food, clothing, and money. They have so far overcome death that many of them now living are over 500 years old...." Full of uplifting ideas. They explain how they do it and how you can do the same.

Psychological Immortality
Jerry Gillies

$12.95, cloth, 256 pages
Richard Marek, New York, NY
A synthesis of science and immortalist philosophy. Exercises to expand aliveness.

Hariakhan Baba: Known, Unknown
Hari Dass

$2.50, paper
Sri Rama Foundation, Davis, CA
Hariakhan Baba is an immortal master of India. He has appeared for thousands of years throughout the Himalayan districts. This book contains stories, interviews and photographs never before published in the West; 18 photographs.

Suggested Listening

Spiritual Psychology

As A Man Thinketh
Leonard Orr

$12.00

Approximately one hour cassette

Produced by Life Unlimited (see address below)

Recorded positive version of James Allen's classic essay on the power of thought in all areas of life. Designed for repeated listening. Use this tape as a tool for self-analysis and as an affirmation.

Also available: AS A WOMAN THINKETH is the same essay with a woman's voice and pronouns. (also $12.00)

Rebirthing

Recreating Your Ideal Birth
Rima Beth Star and Glen Smyly

$15.00

30 Minutes each side.

Produced by Life Unlimited (see address below)

This is a cassette tape of a guided visualization process with a music background. It starts with relaxation, leading you back in time prior to conception. You then picture your conception, growth in the womb, birth and post birth experiences in the way you would like them to have been. Side Two is filled with affirmations on forgiveness and healing of your birth experience.

The Rebirth Seminar
Leonard Orr

$18.00, 2 One hour cassette tapes (Live)
Produced by Life Unlimited (see address below)
The complete rebirth se inar, given in February 1977 by Leonard Orr, inventor of rebirthing and founder of Theta Seminars. Includes: What rebirthing is. The purpose and results of being rebirthed. How rebirthing was invented. What to expect in being rebirthed. Suggested follow up. Life energy and breathing. The breathing release. Healing, health and rebirthing. How rebirthing works. A model of the mind. The Rebirth seminar is a recommended prerequisite for being rebirthed. The tape is valuable whether or not you plan to be rebirthed.

Birth Separation
Barrie Konicov

$10.00
This is a cassette tape 45 minutes on a side.
The titles available on side two of the tape are GOOD HEALTH or PARENTAL DISAPPROVAL. The birth experience for most people is very traumatic. It can be the source of many physical ailments. This tape will help correct your breathing and release the negative feelings of your past that surround your birth. This hypnotic tape is designed for repeated use.

Good Health
Barrie Konicov

$10.00
Cassette tape, 45 minutes on a side.
This is a guided visualization hypnotic tape designed to improve your health. Those that have used it report amazing changes in their health, both mentally and physically. There are many titles available on side two. The most popular are BIRTH SEPARATION and TELL YOUR FEELINGS HOW TO FEEL.

Money and Prosperity

Money Seminar
Leonard Orr

$30.00
Produced by Life Unlimited (see address below)
4 tape set, Over 4 hours (Recorded Live)
These ideas have doubled and tripled the incomes of hundreds of people. The tapes include: The four laws of wealth. The most valuable idea in the universe. The relationship between money and love. What a prosperity consciousness is, and how to develop it. How to increase your income while doing what you enjoy most. Practical tools to have and enjoy any level of prosperity you desire. Dealing with bills. Spending. The savings principle. Keys to investing in stocks and real estate. The best investment there is. Prosperity affirmations. Financial independence — what it is and how to achieve it. How to end taxes. This tape may be used repetitively as a tool in mastering prosperity consciousness. It will pay for itself.

Money and the Five Biggies
Leonard Orr

$18.00
Two one-hour cassettes
Produced by Life Unlimited (see address below)
Leonard's classic money seminar, recorded live at the Rolf Institute. Includes using your mind to produce prosperity, the five basic blocks to wealth, and how to attain success consciousness. Plus valuable hints on budgeting, spending, saving, investing and prospering.

Live Long and Prosper
Jerry Gillies

$59.95, 12 Part Album
A 12 part course in abundance and success on 6 cassettes featuring Jerry Gillies, with all-new material inspired by his bestselling books, MONEYLOVE and PSYCHOLOGICAL IMMORTALITY. Includes: A SENSE OF PURPOSE; THE SUCCESS HABIT; THE CREATIVE SELF; DECISION/COMMITMENT: FINANCIAL SELF CONFIDENCE; TAKE YOUR TIME; VISUALIZING SUCCESS, and a report packed with ideas for CREATIVE CASSETTE LISTENING. These tapes really work!

Your Ideal Relationship With Money
Sondra Ray

$10.00   Approximately 30 Minutes/side Cassette Tape.
Produced by Life Unlimited (see address below)
Fill your mind with prosperity the easy way with this beautiful affirmations tape. The tape contains Sondra's highest and best ideas about prosperity and money in affirmation form. Repetitive listening (with an open mind) will free you from all financial limitation by bringing up and dissolving any ideas in conflict with the positive ideas presented. The masterful musical background by Raphael makes listening a pleasure and helps to slide the ideas right into your subconscious. This is a wonderful way to practice the prosperity ideas presented in some of our other products. Both sides are identical.

Prosperity Plus
Rev. Ike

$12.00
Full of positive ideas about money. Contains an excellent success and prosperity visualization.

Money Prosperity
Barrie Konicov

$10.00

This is a cassette tape with a day version on one side and a night version on the other. This tape has a relaxation process and a guided visualization on overcoming barriers to success and a series of positive affirmations. It is designed for daily use to build a prosperity consciousness. Begin preparing your consciousness to attract the riches you deserve today!

Physical Immortality

Unravelling The Birth/Death Cycle
by Leonard Orr

$18.00 2 tape set, approximately 2 hours (Live)
Produced by Life Unlimited (see address below)
An excellent tape on 2 of the 5 Biggies: Birth and Death. Why do people die? There is an unconscious link between the patterns set up at birth and the time and circumstances of your death. Death is not inevitable. This powerful tape explores the possibility of unravelling your own programming toward death. You will experience greater aliveness now as you reclaim control over the destiny of your physical body. Depression, failure and hopelessness will become things of the past. Explore youthing as an alternative to aging. Family patterns. The unconscious death urge and how it operates. Affirmations. One of Leonard's best.

Spiritual Purification
Leonard Orr

$18.00

Two cassette tapes (Live), Approximately 3 hours.
Produced by Life Unlimited (see address below)
Specific practical techniques for purifying your body and mind. The benefits and necessity of spiritual purification are discussed. Many of these methods are collected from Leonard's visits with Immortal Masters in India. This is the tape for developing practical mastery over your physical body — the practical side of physical immortality.

Affirmations

Your Ideal Loving Relationship
Sondra Ray / Raphael

$10.00

Approximately 45 Minutes/side Cassette Tape
Produced by Life Unlimited (see address below)
Here is the perfect companion to Sondra's book. Just lie back, relax, switch on the tape player, and listen to incredibly beautiful music accompanied by the highest available positive thoughts on Loving Relationships. This is an affirmations tape, intended for repeated listening. Sondra suggests playing it while lying down, bathing, driving, or anytime you can relax and let it slide into your subconscious. The music was created by Raphael specifically for these affirmations. Those of you who have heard him perform know that he has the ability to capture the exact vibration of an idea, and transmit it through music. Each of his compositions with Sondra uniquely fit the meaning of the affirmations, and blend perfectly into an irresistible harmonious whole. The affirmations cover a full range of relation-

ship ideas — attracting and keeping your perfect partner, fulfillment and depth in the relationship, successful communication, harmony, and support, getting exactly what you want, resolving old patterns, and more. Both sides are identical.

Your Ideal Relationship With Sex
Sondra Ray

$10.00
Approximately 24 Minutes/side Cassette Tape
Produced by Life Unlimited (see address below)
Sexual Pleasure is your divine birthright. This tape is designed by Sondra to free your mind of limiting beliefs about sex, such as guilt, fear, inhibition, etc. Through the use of affirmations, results you can expect include the ability to relax and be yourself freely in sex, freedom to honor your own desires and standards regarding sex. Clarity about your purpose in sex, increased intensity and duration of sexual pleasure, being more comfortable with your sexuality and sensuality and certainty that pleasure, and sex, are good, and divinely approved. Raphael has created a sensual musical background especially for these affirmations. Both sides are identical.

Your Ideal Relationship With Your Body And Weight
Sondra Ray

$10.00
Approximately 24 Minutes/side Cassette Tape
Produced by Life Unlimited (see address below)
This affirmation tape trains your mind to have power over your body and what your body does with the food you eat. You establish the goal of your perfect weight and use those affirmations to bring it into being. You will also learn to love, or expand your love, for your body. The tape includes a specially composed musical background by Raphael. Both sides are identical.

How to Obtain These Books and Tapes

The prices listed above are accurate at the time of this printing, and may change. Many of the books are available in bookstores. To make it easy for you, I have arranged with LIFE UNLIMITED to carry all of the products listed above.

Write or call for a free catalog:
LIFE UNLIMITED
8125 Sunset Ave., Suite #204E
Fair Oaks, CA 95628
(916) 967-8442

To order the products listed above:
1. List the titles you want,
2. Include your name and shipping address,
3. Add $1.75 for shipping and handling plus .35¢ per title.
4. California residents add sales tax.
5. Make your check or money order to
LIFE UNLIMITED.
(Checks must be drawn on a U.S. bank.)

Or call and charge it (Visa or Mastercard). There is a 4% handling fee on telephone orders.

*

Readers interested in obtaining information on Rebirthing or LRT should write the following addresses:

For information concerning LRT and Sondra Ray
LRT
145 West 87th Street
New York, NY 10024
(212) 799-7323 — 7324

For information concerning Rebirthing in your area call:

Rebirth International
(1-800-641-4645) ext. 232